TOP 200 Vegan Recipes Coo

Written by: Jamie Stewart

Copyright © 2015

All Rights Reserved

All rights reserved. No part of this book may be reproduced or transmitted in any form or by any means, electronic or mechanical, including photocopying, recording or by any information storage and retrieval system, without written permission from the publisher, except for the inclusion of brief quotations in a review.

Warning-Disclaimer

The purpose of this book is to educate and entertain. The author or publisher does not guarantee that anyone following the techniques, suggestions, tips, ideas, or strategies will become successful. The author and publisher shall have neither liability or responsibility to anyone with respect to any loss or damage caused, or alleged to be caused, directly or indirectly by the information contained in this book.

Table Of Contents

Why Vegan?

There are too many reasons to go vegan. A lot of people are vegans due to the fact they think a meat-free diet is healthy for them. The most of vegans are against cruelty to animals. Those are ethical arguments. Some people believe it's beneficial to the Earth. Those are environmental arguments. Many others are just looking for a change and delicious food. There are a lot of aspects why people become vegan. It does not matter what your personal reasons are. This is the book that can help you with the proper and healthy choices of your daily meals.

How will vegan foods lead to your greater joy?

It does not matter if you are a longtime vegan or a beginner, we cannot skip the discussion about the importance of veganism. If you are an experienced vegan, it's good to remind yourself of this. If you are a beginner, welcome to this wonderful journey!

Veganism is a more than diet. Actually, vegan is a special philosophy and lifestyle. Choosing vegan foods, you choose a different perspective on life and nutrition. A lot of people are becoming increasingly aware and informed about how animal food products are manufactured and chemically processed and in what way it influences our eating and health. We have to be aware of environmental effects of raising animals for food, clothing and other purposes. For many people, it is cruelty to animals, they do not want to participate in this anymore. Therefore, some of them choose veganism as a better path.

Actually, in order to become a vegan, the person must have the clear personal reasons for that. If a decision is made due to fashion or some whim, then it is not a good reason. Good reasons are ethical, religious or health care reasons, as well as the reasons that are promoting the general welfare. Don't forget the tolerance – everyone has the right to choose. For that matter, veganism becomes a real pleasure.

However, the complete elimination of animal products from the diet, without background knowledge, is a bad idea. For this reason, both vegan and meat eater should demonstrate responsibility for their own health. This means, there are no differences – you must take into account the quality and quantity of food you eat on any diet!

Animals are compelled to eat food that is predetermined by evolution. Certainly, we are humans and we are endowed with the ability to think. This is about our health and our responsibility, right? Therefore, we all think a lot about our survival and the survival of our planet. Actually, we are talking about the survival foods! After that, we can talk about pleasure. Education, proper food choices and balanced diet lead to your greater joy! Once you begin to correctly implement the vegan lifestyle, you will prevent the growth of many diseases which are related to the eating of animal products. You will be healthy, full of energy, happy! Your consciousness will be changed! With this book, your journey into the magical world of veganism will be much easier and more beautiful.

Forget "living on a salad" delusions

Nutrition is an important subject. Quality of life depends on it. By eating healthier, you will be able to significantly improve your health and well-being. Even more there is a strong possibility that you will definitely no longer need to take any kind of medications. Anyhow, if you are suffering from a health problem, please consult your doctor.

Before you make a big change in your diet, consult an expert. It could be a doctor or a nutritionist (dietitian). Your body weight, psycho-physical condition, age and other factors are very important and they should not be ignored. It would be good to have usual medical check-ups.

Learn to balance your meals. Initially, you may be confused, and therefore this book is your good and useful "tool". Make sure you know as much as possible about vegan food. There are plenty substitutes for animal products – meat, eggs and milk replacement options. In this cookbook, you will find a many recipes with these delicious substitutes for animal products. Therefore, your meals will always be complete, balanced, healthy and very interesting

Meat substitutes are tofu (also called "meat without bones"), soy protein, tempeh, seitan, beans and so on.

Egg substitutes are silken tofu, applesauce, soy yogurt, flax seeds, banana, potato starch, pumpkin, commercial egg substitute and so on.

Dairy substitutes are plain, sweetened, or unsweetened soy milk, nut milk and rice milk. Buttermilk substitutes are, for example, 1 cup soy milk, nut milk or rice milk plus two teaspoons of lemon juice.

Cheese substitutes are casein-free, soy and nut-based cheese substitutes.

Butter substitutes are vegetable margarine and soy margarine, nut butters, as well as fruit purees.

As you can see, the options are endless. There are so many ways to replace meat, eggs and milk as the traditional ingredients. If you have some concerns, this book can help in a few good ways:

If you make an aware and mindful meal plan, you should be full of energy and healthy. This cookbook can help you to get your eating under control, and you should be safe with your Vegan diet.

If you are wondering how to maintain adequate health with plant-based diet, read this cookbook. The meals in this cookbook have been carefully selected, so you can be sure that you enter the right nutrients.

If you think that learning how to cook vegan meals is hard, this cookbook destroys those prejudices. The recipes in this book are explained in details, step by step, there's no way to go wrong. Stick to the cookbook, and your family and guests will be impressed by your culinary skills.

As far as your budget, do not worry! There are many of vegan meals that are as economical as they are tasty!

Going vegan is easier than ever with the right cookbook

The book consists of two hundred Vegan recipes that are grouped into 4 categories: Breakfast, lunch, dinner and fast snacks. Each recipe includes preparation time, serving size, ingredients, and directions.

Anyway, you will notice – If you prepare the same meal twice, it may not be the same dish. Why? Each time, you will add new spices, and you will add more and more love in your recipes! This book gives you guidelines, and you have a wonderful opportunity to explore new flavors of vegan cuisine.

This cookbook is designed to satisfy the sophisticated taste of the longtime vegans, as well as the beginners who are looking for encouragement, inspiration and recipe ideas.

And finally – you do not have to be vegan to enjoy these delicious recipes! This book is created to provide you with support and motivation.

The more that you read this cookbook, the more things you will know about plant-based diet and all its advantages. You have nothing to worry about, because the books like this can do a lot to help you live a healthy and happy life! So, forget "living on a salad" delusions.

Cooking at home instead of eating out has a lot of advantages. It is worth it, see for yourself:

This cookbook is meant to bring family and friends into the kitchen. This means more family gatherings, more smiles, and more health.

Cooking vegan meals at home saves money. You will see that many of the dishes in this book do not cost so much. Compare that price to the price of a meal at a restaurant or even in a fast food restaurant. You will be surprised.

Cooking at home actually saves time. There are many recipes in this book you will be able to prepare for just 5, 10 or 15 minutes!

Calorie savings is another very appealing reason. By cooking at home, you can control the amount of fat, salt, calories, as well as the size of your portions.

You have nothing to lose, but you can get a lot more! When you start to get to know the beauty of a vegan diet from these recipes, you'll realize that vegans are not deprived. Not at all.

"A man can live and be healthy without killing animals for food; therefore, if he eats meat, he participates in taking animal life merely for the sake of his appetite. And to act so is immoral." Leo Tolstoy said.

Going vegan is easier and healthier than ever before, with our cookbook. We wish you happy cooking! Enjoy every vegan bite!

PART ONE BREAKFAST

Tofu Skillet with Soy Sausage

(Ready in about 15 minutes | Servings 4)

Ingredients

1 pound firm tofu, drained and crumbled

1/4 teaspoon turmeric

1/4 teaspoon salt

1/4 fresh ground pepper

1 teaspoon onion powder

1/2 teaspoon freshly ground black pepper

2 tablespoons vegetable oil

1 small onion, chopped

1 clove garlic, finaly chopped

1/2 cup mushroom, sliced

1 cup meatless soy sausage, sliced

1 tablespoon nutritional yeast flakes

2 teaspoons soy sauce, e.g. tamari

Directions

Combine tofu with turmeric, salt, pepper and onion powder in a medium bowl.

Heat a large skillet over medium heat in first, and then add the vegetable oil. Add the onion and garlic, cook stirring occasionally. Cook until the onions are translucent.

Add the mushrooms and sausage to the skillet and sprinkle with the Yeast flakes. Cook for 5 minutes.

Add the tofu mixture to the skillet and stir well. Drizzle with tamari sauce and cook until the tofu is dry, it is about 5 minutes. Decorate with chopped leeks.

Cranberry and Raisins Soft Bread

(Ready in about 1 hour 30 minute | Servings 6)

Ingredients

2 cups flour

2 teaspoon baking powder

1/2 teaspon baking soda

Pinch of salt, or to taste

1 cup sugar

2 tablespoons margarine, melted

Warm water, as much as it's necessary to get a soft dough

1/2 cup raw cranberries

1/2 cup raisins

Directions

Preheat the oven to 350 F.

Sift the flour, sugar, baking powder, baking soda into a large mixing bowl. Add salt and mix well. Add melted margarine and warm water. Mix well using a wooden spoon.

Add cranberries and raisins. Stir well. Shape the dough in a ball. Place your bread in a covered loaf pan, and put in the middle of the oven shelf. Bake 1 hour.

Hot Sandwich with Tomato

(Ready in about 15 minutes | Servings 1)

Ingredients

1 large tomato, sliced

1 medium cucumber

Whole grain roll

1 tablespoon vegan margarine

Salt to taste

a dash of pepper

3 Olives

Directions

Cut tomato and cucumber into slices. Season to taste.

Arrange vegetables over the bread smeared with margarine.

Toast in a sandwich toaster and serve hot with olives.

Cranberries Oatmeal Waffles

(Ready in about 1 hour | Servings 6)

Ingredients

1 cup whole wheat flour

1 cup quick cooking oats

1 ½ cups cranberries

1/4 teaspoon fresh ground Jamaica pepper

1 tablespoon baking powder

1/3 cup unsweetened applesauce

1 ½ cups unsweetened rice milk

3 tablespoons maple syrup

2 tablespoons neutral vegetable oil

1 teaspoon vanilla paste

Directions

Stir flour, baking powder, Jamaica pepper and salt into a mixing bowl. Stir in the oats.

Make a hole in the center and gradually mix rice milk, maple syrup, oil, applesauce, and vanilla. Mix all ingredients together to make slightly sticky dough..

Leave for 10 minutes. Put cranberries on the top.

Cook in a waffle iron. Brush your waffle iron with oil between each waffle, optionally. The waffles thickness will depend on waffle iron size, so choose your favourite size.

Easy Green Smoothie

(Ready in about 10 minutes | Servings 1)

Ingredients

2 handfuls of spinach

2 celery sticks

1 small slice fresh ginger, peeled

1 pear, peeled and sliced

1 tablespoon chia seeds

1/2 cup water

ice cubes to taste or freeze pear

1 teaspoon unflavored vitamin C crystals

Directions

Put spinach leaves into an electric blender.

Add water and blend together until all spinach leaves are finely chopped.

Put celery, ginger, pear and chia seeds, and turn your blender to 'high'. Add vitamin C. Blend again until smooth. You can add ice cubes if you want.

Pour into a large cup of your choice.

Light Summer Smoothie

(Ready in about 10 minutes | Servings 1)

Ingredients

1 large peach

1 medium nectarine

1 large banana

1 cup water

4 figs

3 cubes ice

Directions

Place all ingredients in an electric blender. Blend until the ingredients are smooth. You need to get bit-free consistency.

Add ice cubes or use frozen fruits. Decorate with strawberries.

Blueberry Muffins

(Ready in about 40 minutes Servings | 6)

Ingredients

2 ½ cups brown spelt flour	1 teaspoon cinnamon, ground
4 tablespoons tapioca, ground	2 tablespoons vegetable oil
2 cups frozen blueberries	7 tablespoons unsweetened applesauce
1/4 cup flax seeds, ground	1 cup maple syrup
Pinch of salt	1 tablespoons vanilla extract
3 teaspoons baking powder	1/2 cup water

Directions

Preheat the oven to 400 degrees F. Use non-stick 12 cup muffin pan for baking.

Sift flour, tapioca, flax seeds, baking powder, and cinnamon together. Stir in frozen blueberries. Add remaining ingredients and stir into the mixture.

Bake for 20 minutes in the muffin pan.

Winter Fruit Salad

(Ready in about 10 minutes | Servings 1)

Ingredients

1 ½ cup fresh cranberries, washed

1 big apple, peeled and diced

1/3 cup orange juice

1/4 cup raisins, chopped

1 tablespoons honey or molasses

Directions

You need to grind cranberries first for about 1 minute.

Then add remaining ingredients and mix well. Pour orange juice over fruit.

You can refrigerate salad for 1 hour. Stir again before serving.

Bowl of Tropical Fruit Salad

(Ready in about 25 minutes | Servings 4)

Ingredients

2 cups grapes, seedless

1 banana, peeled and sliced

2 medium kiwis, peeled and sliced

2 tablespoons lime juice

2 cans (2 ½ cups) pineapple chunks, unsweetened

1 mango, peeled and chopped

1 small pineapple, cored and chopped

3/4 cup coconut flakes, sweetened

2 tablespoons coconut nectar

Directions

Preheat the oven to 350 degrees F. Put the coconut flakes on a baking sheet. Bake until golden, or about 5 minutes. Put coconut flakes into small bowl and cool.

Mix together the coconut nectar and lime juice for dressing.

Add the grapes, banana, kiwis, pineapple and mango. Make sure that all the ingredients are coated with the dressing. Before serving, sprinkle with the additional coconut flakes.

Wake-Me-Up Fruit Compote

(Ready in about 45 minutes | Servings 4)

Ingredients

1 ½ cup water

1/2 cup dried apricots, chopped

12 medium apples, peeled, cored and diced

4 large peaches, diced

2/3 cup coconut flakes

1 tablespoon lemon zest

3 tablespoons ginger juice, fresh

a dash of cinnamon

Directions

Use a large pot and pour water.

Add dried apricots and cook until they are tender. Add apple and peaches.

Cook it for a while, fruit should be soft.

Add coconut flakes and water. Add lemon zest. Cook a few more minutes to the dried coconut flakes become soft. Turn off heat and then add the ginger juice and cinnamon to taste. Serve warm.

Sunday Morning Pancakes

(Ready in about 40 minutes | Servings 4)

Ingredients

2 ½ cups brown rice flour

1 cup soy flour

Pinch of salt

3 teaspoons baking powder

1/2 cup macadamia nuts and pecans mix, chopped

1/4 cup Canola Oil

3 cups soy milk

1/4 cup maple syrup

3 tablespoons orange zest

A few dried figs to taste

Directions

Preheat the oven to 400 degrees F. Use non-stick muffin pan.

Mix both types of flour together. Add baking powder and salt. Then stir in and toasted macadamia nuts and pecans.

Whisk oil, soy milk, and orange zest and add into the flour mixture.

Cook pancakes on a preheated griddle pan.

Serve with maple syrup, figs and your favorite fruits.

Quick Garlicky Hummus

(Ready in about 10 minutes | Servings 6)

Ingredients

4 garlic cloves, peeled

3 cups beans, cooked

2 tablespoons lemon juice

2 tablespoons tahini

1 teaspoon mustrard

1/4 teaspoon cumin

1 tablespoon miso, light

Salt to taste

Cayenne pepper to taste

Directions

Place all ingredients, except salt, to a food processor (or blender) and blend until the mixture is smooth. Start the blender on low and progressively increase speed to high.

Stop the blender and taste your hummus. Ada salt to taste. If you want, you can add more seasonings. Blend for a few minutes to mix well.

Store hummus in a covered container in your refrigerator.

Mushroom Pâté with Herbs

(Ready in about 30 minutes | Servings 6)

Ingredients

2 pounds fresh mushrooms, finely chopped

4 cloves garlic, minced

1 red onion, chopped

1 tablespoon margarine

2 tablespoons fresh parsley, chopped

1 ½ cups bread crumbs

1 tbsp lemon juice

Salt to taste

1 teaspoon ground pepper

Directions

Heat the margarine in a sauce pan before frying the onions. Stir fry the onions for 5-6 minutes, or until it is translucent.

Add the mushroom and cook for another 8-10 minutes. Remove from the heat.

Add garlic, herbs and lemon juice. Season with salt and pepper. Replace the mixture to an electric blender, until very soft.

Almond Pâté Vegan Style

(Ready in about 30 minutes | Servings 4)

Ingredients

1 cup almonds

1 tablesppon lemon juice (freshly squeezed)

1 teaspoon vegetable oil

1 teaspoon tamari soy sauce

Salt to taste

dash of cayenne

1 stalk celery

fresh parsley to taste, finaly chopped

2 tablespoons garlic, peeled and minced

1 tablespoon onion, minced

1 tablespoon fresh basil

Directions

Process almonds, garlic, lemon juice, oil, tamari sauce, celery and salt in a food processor or electric blender, until the mixture has become creamy.

Transfer to a small bowl. Add seasoning and onion and mix well.

Chill before serving.

Skinny Girl Vegetable Pâté

(Ready in about 1 hour 20 minutes |Servings 4)

Ingredients

1 large potato, peeled and chopped

1 large carrot peeled and chopped

1 cup sunflower seeds

1/2 cup whole wheat flour

1/2 cup nutritional yeast

1/2 teaspoon tsp salt

1/2 cup extra-virgin olive oil

1 tablespoon lemon juice

1 onion, funaly chopped

1 clove garlic, peeled

1 ½ cups water

1/2 teaspoon dried thyme

1/2 teaspoon basil, dried

1/2 teaspoon black pepper, ground

1 teaspoon dry mustard

Directions

Preheat oven to 350 degrees F.

Process sunflower seeds, flour, nutritional yeast, salt, oil, lemon juice, potato, carrot, onion, garlic, water, thyme, basil, pepper and dry mustard in an electric blender. Blend till the mixture has become creamy.

Place your mixture to the baking dish.

Bake in the preheated oven 1 hour, or until it has become brown.

Chill before serving.

Toasted Green Bean Sandwich

(Ready in about 20 minutes | Servings 2)

Ingredients

2 tablespoons vegan sour cream

1 tablespoon vegan mayonnaise

1/4 cup alfalfa sprouts

1/4 cup parsley

1/4 cup marinated green beans, cooked and drained

1/4 cup hummus

1/4 red onion, thinly sliced

1/4 cup radish sprouts

1/4 teaspoon fresh oregano

2 slices sourdough bread

Directions

Mix Sour cream and mayonnaise with alfalfa sprouts in a small mixing bowl. Stir parsley into dressing. Spread the dressing evenly on both slices of bread.

Spread the hummus evenly. Layer the green beans, onion, and radish. Sprinkle with oregano. Top with the other piece of bread.

Toast in preheated oven for 5 minutes. Serve hot.

Tofu Sour Cream

(Ready in about 15 minutes | Serving 4)

Ingredients

3/4 cup extra-firm tofu, drained

1/4 cup raw cashews, finaly ground

1 tablespoon white rice vinegar

1 tablespoon lemon juice

1 tablespoon white miso

1 tablespoon vegetable oil

Directions

Process all ingredients in an electric blender or a food processor.

Blend until your mixture is smooth and very creamy.

This Tofu Sour Cream will stay fresh for 7 days if it is stored in the freezer.

Delicious Mango Muffins

(Ready in about 1 hour | Servings 12)

Ingredients

1/2 cup mango chutney

1/4 cup tahini (or hummus with peanut butter)

1 tablespoon sesame oil

2 teaspoons coriander, ground

1 cup rice milk unsweetened

1 ¾ cups whole wheat pastry flour

2 teaspoons baking powder

A pinch of salt

Directions

Preheat oven to 350 degrees F.

Mix mango chutney, tahini, and sesame oil. Add coriander and milk. Sift flour, baking powder, and salt.

Transfer mixture in a muffin pan. Bake for 40 minutes

How to test a muffin to see if it is done? You should insert toothpick into the center of a muffin. It should be baked when the toothpick comes out clean.

Quick Soft Bread

(Ready in about 1 hour 10 minutes | Servings 12)

Ingredients

1 cup quick oats

1 cup whole wheat pastry flour

1 cup bread flour

1/2 cup non-dairy butter

1/2 cup unsweetened applesauce

1 cup almond milk

1 tablespoon baking powder

Salt ot taste

A few pecans, sliced

Directions

Preheat oven to 375 degrees F.

Mix butter, applesauce, and almond milk in a microwave-safe bowl. Heat for 40 seconds.

Whisk quick oats, both of flours, baking powder, and salt.

Transfer dough into prepared baking pan. Sprinkle sliced pecans on top.

Bake for 55 minutes. You should insert toothpick into the center of the bread. It should be baked until the toothpick comes out clean.

Homemade Flaky Biscuits

(Ready in about 40 minutes | Servings 12)

Ingredients

1 ½ cups granola

1 ½ cups all-purpose pastry flour

1/4 cup non-dairy butter

2 tablespoons honey

1/4 cup almond milk

2 teaspoons baking powder

Salt to taste

2 tablespoons rice or almond milk

Directions

Preheat oven to 375 degrees F.

Process granola, flour, baking powder, salt, butter, and honey in your electric blender.

Stir in milk and knead dough gently, until it feels like elastic to fingers.

Roll out to 1/2-in. thickness. Cut with a 2-1/2-in. cookie cutter and place on a baking sheet which is lined with parchment paper.

Bake for 14 to 16 minutes until biscuits are golden.

Quick Vegan French Toast

(Ready in about 25 minutes | Servings 2)

Ingredients

4 slices bread	1 cup unsweetened non-dairy milk
1 tablespoon chia seeds	A dash of cinnamon
1 tablespoon flax seed, ground	4-5 raspberries
1/2 tablespoon maple syrup	whipped coconut cream, if desired

Directions

Combine seeds, maple syrup, milk and cinnamon in a large mixing bowl. Place in the fridge for about 20 minutes.

Preheat griddle to medium heat, to 350 degrees F, and grease with coconut oil.

Dip your slices of bread into the batter on each side, by checking to make sure it's fully submerged.

Place on griddle and cook until evenly golden brown. Then flip and cook the other side for about 4 minutes.

Decorate: Top with coconut whipped cream and raspberries. Add extra maple syrup if desired.

Quick Spiced Nuts

(Ready in about 10 minutes | Servings 4)

Ingredients

2 tablespoon mild flavored oil

2 teaspoons chili powder

1 ½ cup mixed nuts such as almonds, walnuts, Brazil nuts

1/3 cup raw pistachios

4 tablespoons dark soy sauce

Sea salt to taste

Directions

Heat the oil in a wok. Add the chili powder. Cook over a high heat for about 1 minute, stirring permanently.

Add the nuts and pistachios toss them in the oil and chili. Mix to coat nuts evenly. Fry the nuts for 1 minute.

Add the soy sauce to the wok and cook for about 3 minutes, until all the sauce has evaporated

Sprinkle a little salt over the nuts and serve dried.

Muskmelon with crunchy seeds

(Ready in about 25 minutes | Servings 6)

Ingredients

1 big Muskmelon

1 cup pumpkin seeds

4 tablespoons vegetable oil

Salt to taste

1/2 teaspoon black pepper, ground

Directions

Preheat the oven to 350° degrees F.

Combine the pumpkin seeds with the olive oil in a bowl, then transfer them on a baking sheet. Sprinkle a little salt over them.

Put it in the middle of the oven shelf and bake for about 10 minutes. Sprinkle with pepper.

Cut the muskmelon in a halves, and scoop out the seeds with a dessert spoon. Cut each half lengthwise into 2 segments. Then cut the flesh into bite-size chunks. Sprinkle the crunchy seasoned seeds over melon chunks.

Breakfast Smoothie To Go

(Ready in about 5 minutes | Servings 1)

Ingredients

1 apple, washed, peeled and cored

1 banana, peeled

1/2 cup frozen peaches or mango

1/3 cup raw Brasil nuts

1 tablespoon flax seeds

2 ½ cups hemp milk

1/3 cup soy non-diary yogurt without sugar

Algae powder or liquid to taste

Ice cubes to taste

Directions

Pour the liquids in your electric blender. Add fresh fruit, nuts and then add frozen fruit. Then add the rest of the ingredients. In the end, add ice cubes.

Start at a lower speed. Then increase the speed slowly.

Blend until smooth.

Winter Hummus Sandwich

(Ready in about 10 minutes | Servings 1)

Ingredients

1 whole-grain bun

1/4 cup hummus

1 small pickled cucumber

1⁄4 cup beets, canned and sliced

1/4 teaspoon cumin

1 large lettuce leaf

1 tablespoon Vegan mayonnaise

Directions

Cut a bun lengthwise. Spread the hummus evenly on your bun.

Add vegan eggless mayonnaise.

Layer the cucumbers, beets and lettuce. Sprinkle with cumin.

Extra tip: Toast the bread for winter days.

Hot Quinoa Porridge

(Ready in about 15 minutes | Servings 4)

Ingredients

1 cup quinoa

1⁄3 cup vanilla soy or hemp milk

2 teaspoons brown sugar

1⁄4 teaspoon ground cinnamon

1⁄4 cup sunflower seeds

Salt to taste

dried raisins to taste

Directions

Heat a medium saucepan over law-medium heat. Mix all ingredients in a saucepan.

Cook slowly over medium heat about 10 minutes, stirring frequently.

Add more water if it is required to prevent burning and sticking. Serve hot.

Quick Rice Porridge

(Ready in about 15 minutes | Servings 4)

Ingredients

1 cup brown rice

1/4 cup water

1 teaspoon soy sauce

1/4 cup pumpkin seeds

1 cup bok choy, sliced

Directions

In a medium saucepan bring water to the boil, and then stir in rice.

Cook for about 10 minutes. Whisk and bring to a low simmer over medium heat.

Add the seeds, bok choy and soy sauce. Cover and simmer for 5 minutes.

Kale Hash Breakfast Treat

(Ready in about 45 minutes | Servings 4)

Ingredients

1/4 cup vegetable oil

2 tablespoons soy sauce

1 tablespoon vinegar

1 teaspoon black pepper, ground

1 teaspoon cayenne pepper

1 teaspoon mustard, dried

1/2 cup kale, chopped

1 cup potatoes, grated

1/2 cup red onion, finaly chopped

2 garlic cloves, minced

1 teaspoon basil

1/4 cup nutritional yeast flakes

2 cups marinated tofu, crumbled

Directions

Preheat the oven to 350 degrees F.

Line the cookie sheet with parchment paper.

Mix vegetable oil, soy sauce, vinegar, pepper, cayenne pepper and dried mustard in a large bowl. Stir well.

Add the kale, potatoes, onion, garlic, basil, yeast and marinated tofu.

Place the mixture over the cookie sheet evenly. Bake for about 40 minutes. Serve warm.

Winter Veggie Hash

(Ready in about 30 minutes | Servings: 4)

Ingredients

1 cup hash brown

1/2 cup butternut squash cubed

2 small bell pepper, seeded and diced

1/2 cup cauliflower, chopped

1 small onion, peeled and chopped

1 garlic cloves, peeled and minced

1 tablespoon olive oil

Freshly ground black pepper

3/4 teaspoon kosher salt

Directions

Prepare the hashbrowns according to instructions on a package.

In a medium sauce pan, cook the vegetables until soft. Add salt and pepper.

Serve hot on a plate with a chopped parsley.

Homemade Cornbread Muffins

(Ready in about 40 minutes | Servings 12)

Ingredients

6 tablespoons water

2 tablespoons flax seeds, ground

1 cup corn flour

1/2 cup all purpose flour

1/2 cup unbleached white flour

1/4 cup rapadura sugar

4 teaspoons baking powder

1/4 cup shredded apple

1 cup vanilla soy milk, unsweetened

1/4 cup safflower oil

3/4 teaspoon salt

1/4 teaspoon grated nutmeg

Directions

Preheat the oven to 425 degrees F.

Spray the muffin pan (muffin cups) with your favorite non-stick pan spray.

Bring a water to the boil in a saucepan over medium-high heat. Add the flax seeds. Simmer for 2 minutes.

Sift the flours, rapadura sugar, baking powder, apples, and into a large bowl. Mix well. Combine the milk, oil, salt and nutmeg in another mixing bowl, and whisk all together. Stir in flax seeds mixture.

Add this liquid mixture to the dry (flour) mixture. Stir until smooth. Transfer the dough to the muffin cups and bake.

Bake for about 15 minutes. Set aside to cool before serving.

Healthy Veggie Chips

(Ready in about 25 minutes | Servings 4)

Ingredients

1 bunch of curly kale, washed and dried

1 celery root, peeled and halved crosswise

2 teaspoons nutritional yeast flakes

2 tablespoons vegetable oil

2 teaspoons apple cider vinegar

1/4 teapoon thyme

1 teaspoon sea salt

Directions

Preheat the oven to 425 degrees F.

Place sliced kale and celery on a baking sheet. Sprinkle with yeast. Bake for 6 minutes.

Combine the vegetable oil, vinegar, thyme and salt in a mixing bowl. Toss the vegetables in the liquid mixture.

After the one side starts to brown, toss the vegetables on the baking sheet and bake the other side up for 3 minutes.

Green Spiced Polenta

(Ready in about 2 hours | Servings 6)

Ingredients

1 ½ cups non-diary milk

1 ½ cups water

1/4 cup vegetable oil

1 cup cornmeal

1/2 cup seitan, diced

1/2 cup onion, diced

1 clove garlic, minced

1 pound greens, fresh and dried

1/2 teaspoon salt

1 cup Tofu cheese

1/2 tsp paprika (optional)

1/2 tsp cumin powder

Directions

Preheat the oven to 425 degrees F.

Line a baking pan with a parchment paper.

Mix the non-diary milk, water, and 1/2 teaspoon of salt in a medium saucepan, and bring to a simmer over medium heat.

Pour the cornmeal into the pot, stirring frequently. Turn the heat to low and cook for 5 minutes, whisking constantly. Stir the vegetable oil into the cooked polenta.

Transfer the polenta into the prepared baking pan. Sprinkle with a pinch of salt. Cover the mixture with a clean kitchen towel and let it cool in the refrigerator, at least 1 hour.

Then bake for 30 minutes, or until golden on top.

Meanwile, heat a large pot. Sautee the seitan, onion, garlic, and a pinch of salt for about 8 minutes. Add greens to the pot and cook until the leaves are well wilted. Add paprika and cumin powder.

Remove the polenta from the oven. Add the Tofu Cheese on top evenly, and then

spread the seitan and greens mixture on top. Bake briefly for 3 minutes.

Fluffy Easy Bread

(Ready in about 2 hours 50 minutes | Servings 6)

Ingredients

4 cups unbleached flour

1 (or 2 ¼ teaspoon) packet dry yeast

1 teaspoon salt

2 tablespoons semi-flavored vegetable oil

1 ¾ cups hot water

Directions

Combine flour, salt, and yeast in a mixing bowl. Then form a hole in the bottom. Add water and the vegetable oil. Mix slowly. Shape in a ball.

Transfer on a work surface (previously floured). Knead the dough for 5 minutes, until the mixture becomes elastic. Transfer the dough in a large bowl, cover with a clean kitchen towel, and let rise in a warm place. Leave for about 1 hour.

Knead the dough again to work out air bubbles, ant let it rise 20 minutes more.

Preheat oven to 375 degrees F. Bake for about 40 minutes, until your bread develops golden color.

Cauliflower & Broccoli Croquettes

(Ready in about 2 hours | Servings 6)

Ingredients

2 tablespoons vegetable oil

2 cloves garlic, peeled minced

1 teaspoon dried tarragon

1/4 ground black pepper

1/2 teaspoon salt

1 cup millet

2 ½ cups vegetable soup

2 cups cauliflower, finaly chopped

2 cups broccoli, finaly chopped

Directions

Heat a pot over medium heat. Heat the oil and sauté the garlic for about 30 seconds. Add the tarragon, black pepper, and salt, stirring often. Add the millet and cook for about 3 minutes to toast it.

Add the soup and bring to a boil. Then cook over low heat to a simmer, for 10 minutes.

Stir in the chopped cauliflower and broccoli, and cook for about 15 minutes, stirring constantly. Once the water is mostly absorbed, turn off the heat and continue to cook for 15 minutes more. The millet must be well cooked.

Transfer to a mixing bowl and let cool for a few minutes, then move the bowl to the fridge to cool for about 50 minutes.

Once the mixture is cooled, form it into small balls. Press them down by hand to flatten, and form croquettes.

Heat a large non-stick skillet. Fry the croquettes for 3 minutes on each side, until golden brown.

Crusty-Chewy Bread with Millet

(Ready in about 1 hour 30 minutes | Servings 12)

Ingredients

1 teaspoon Safflower oil

1/2 cup millet, uncooked

1 cup warm water

1½ cups raisins

2 ½ cups white whole wheat flour

1 tablespoon baking powder

2 teaspoons baking soda

A dash of cinnamon

A pinch of salt

1/2 cup vegan margarine

1/3 cup brown sugar

1½ teaspoons apple cider vinegar

1¼ cups non-diary milk

Directions

Preheat the oven to 375 degrees F.

Heat a sauce pan and add the oil. Heat over medium heat and add the millet. Cook for 2 to 3 minutes.

Pour in the boiling water, stir in the raisins, and cook 20 minutes, until the liquid is evaporated. Cool the millet mixture to room temperature.

Then prepare a dough. Sift the flour, baking powder, baking soda, cinnamon and salt in a large mixing bowl. Stir in the margarine and sugar.

Combine milk and vinegar, then set aside to sit for a minute, to curdle. Stir the curdled milk and the millet mixture into the flour mixture. Knead the dough to form a dense ball. Make sure do not overwork the dough.

Transfer the ball of dough into the baking pan, and shape into a round loaf. Brush the top of bread loaf with soy milk.

Bake for 45 minutes. You should insert toothpick into the center of the bread. It should be baked until the toothpick comes out clean.

Quick Grilled Polenta

(Ready in about 30 minutes | Servings 4)

Ingredients

1 tablespoon kosher salt

2 cups polenta

2 tablespoons vegetable oil

Directions

Pour water in a medium pot and add the salt. Then add polenta and whisk in.

Bring to a boil over high heat, and add oil. Turn the heat right down and cook, stirring constantly using a wooden spoon. Stir for a few minutes, until it thickens.

Pour into a glass mold, and cut into pieces with a wet knife.

Grill on a hot non-stick grill on each side, until golden brown.

Cold Tofu Salad Pita

(Ready in about 10 minutes | Servings 4)

Ingredients

1 pound firm tofu

1 teaspoon mustard

1/4 cup soy mayonnaise

2 leeks, chopped

1 small green bell pepper, diced

2 whole wheat pitas

1 tomato, sliced

1 cucumber, sliced

Directions

Crumble tofu in a mixing bowl. Add a mustard, and mayonnaise and mix well.

Add leeks and bell pepper, then stir until well mixed. Cut the pita into halves. Add tofu salad mixture evenly among the pita halves.

Add lettuce, tomatoes, and cucumbers.

Make 4 sandwiches and serve immediately.

Vegetable Tofu Mozzarella Pita

(Ready in about 10 minutes + 8 hours for cooling | Servings 4)

Ingredients

1/2 cup cooked chickpeas

1/2 cup fresh mushrooms

1/4 cup Balsamic Vinaigrette

1 medium tomato, finely diced

1 large green bell pepper, cuted into thin strips

1 small cucumber, finely chopped

1 teaspoon flax seeds, ground

3 ounces tofu mozzarella o

1 whole wheat pita

Directions

Combine the chickpeas and mushrooms with the Balsamic Vinaigrette in a mixing bowl. Cool in refrigerator 8 hours.

Toss the vegetables, flax seeds and tofu with the chickpeas mixture.

Cut the pita into halves. Add the Vegetable Tofu Mozzarella mixture evenly among the pita halves.

Spanish-Style Breakfast

(Ready in about 45 minutes | Servings 4)

Ingredients

2 tablespoons canola oil	1 pound seitan, chopped
1/2 cup onion, chopped	1/4 teaspoons salt
2 teaspoons garlic, peeled minced	1/4 teaspoons black pepper
1 teaspoon cayenne	1/4 teaspoon oregano
2 teaspoons paprika	1/2 cup dry red wine
	1 tablespoon tamari sauce

Directions

Heat the canola oil in a skillet over medium heat. Sauté the onion, garlic, cayenne and paprika until the onion is translucent. Add the seitan.

Add the wine and tamari sauce to the pan and cook until the liquid is absorbed. Remove the pan from the heat. Season, cool the mixture and then form the sausages.

Heat canola oil in a skillet over medium heat, and cook the sausages until well browned.

Peasant Tempeh Sausages

(Ready in about 1 hour 40 minutes | Servings 4)

Ingredients

2 packages tempeh, (8-ounce each) diced

Warm water

1/2 cup all-purpose flour

1/2 teaspoon thyme

11/2 teaspoons sage, rubbed

1/2 teaspoon dried mustard

1/2 teaspoon black pepper

1 tablespoon soy sauce

1/3 cup canola oil

Directions

Steam the tempeh over simmering water for 15 minutes. Set aside for 15 minutes. Drain.

Crumble the tempeh and add the spices. Whisk well. Add the flour, soy sauce, and canola oil and mix well.

Let the sausage mixture rest for a few minutes. Shape the sausage into 8 patties. Put the patties onto a baking sheet, which is lined with parchment paper. Chill for 1 hour.

Cook the formed sausages in a frying-pan over medium heat for 5 minutes on each side.

Serve warm with vegan mayonnaise.

Yukon Gold Potatoes Hash

(Ready in about 40 minutes | Servings 4)

Ingredients

1 ½ pounds Yukon Gold potatoes

1 Bay leaf

1 medium onion, peeled

3 cloves garlic, peeled

2 tablespoon extra-virgin Olive Oil

1/2 teaspoon Kosher Sea

1/4 freshly ground black pepper

Directions

Wash and scrub potatoes. Put the potatoes in a pot of salted water. Bring the water to a boil and cook the potatoes until they are about half done. Cool potatoes. Peel potatoes and cut into slices.

Cut the onion into slices. Chop the garlic cloves as thinly as possible. Heat olive oil in a skillet over medium heat.

Add the onions and garlic in an even layer on the bottom of the pan.

Top it with the potato slices. Add Bay leaf, salt and pepper.

Cook for 15 - 20 minutes, stirring occasionally.

Fluffy Honey Pancakes

(Ready in about 30 minutes | Servings 6)

Ingredients

2 cups all-purpose flour

1 teaspoon baking soda

2 teaspoons baking powder

A pinch of salt

2 tablespoons honey

2 tablespoons applesauce

1 cup non-diary milk

1/2 cup apple juice

2 tablespoons canola oil

2 bananas

2 tablespoons raisins

Directions

Mix the flour, baking soda, baking powder, and salt in a bowl. Add the honey, applesauce, milk, apple juice, and canola oil. Stir until smooth.

Heat a pancake skillet over medium heat. You can use nonstick cooking spray.

Cook the pancakes until bubbles form on the tops and the edges appear firm.

Turn the pancakes using a spatula. Cook until the pancakes are puffed and golden.

Serve warm with bananas and raisins.

Almond-Pecan Smoothie Dream

(Ready in about 15 minutes | Servings 4)

Ingredients

3/4 cup almonds

1/4 cup pecans

3 1/2 cups water

3 dates

2 tablespoons dried cranberries

1 vanilla bean, roughly chopped

2-3 raspberries

1/4 cup alfalfa sprouts

Directions

Soak almonds and pecans in the water overnight. Mix almonds and pecans in a bowl and pour the water.

Rinse and drain the soaked nuts. Place them in an electric blender. Add dates, dried cranberries, alfalfa sprouts and vanilla bean.

Process the mixture on highest speed for 1-2 minutes.

Slowly pour the milk mixture into the nut milk bag. Gently squeeze to release the milk. Cool in the fridge. Decorate with raspberries.

Quick Berry Muesli

(Ready in about 5 minutes | Servings 1)

Ingredients

1 tablespoon pumpkin seeds

1 tablespoon hemp seeds

1/4 cup walnuts, sliced

1/4 cup coconut flakes

1/4 cranberries

1/4 cup blueberries

1 cup non-diary milk

Directions

Combine the seeds, nuts, and coconut, and mix well.

Add the berries.

Cover with non-diary milk and serve immediately.

Strawberry-Chocolate Smoothie

(Ready in about 15 minutes | Servings 1)

Ingredients

1 cup frozen strawberries

2 tablespoons coconut milk

1 frozen banana

1 ½ tablespoons raw cacao powder

3/4 cup water

1/4 cup alfalfa sprouts

Directions

Process all ingredients in a blender, by using high-speed.

Blend until they are thick and smooth.

Add ice cubes to taste and decorate with grated chocolate and strawberries.

Extra tip: For better results, peel your bananas before freezing.

Hummus Sandwich with Arugula

(Ready in about 15 minutes | Servings 2)

Ingredients

1 (14-ounce) can chickpeas, drained and rinsed

3 cloves garlic, peeled and minced

1/4 teaspoon ground coriander

1 tablespoon toasted pumpkin seeds

1/4 cup olive oil

1/4 cup tahini

1/4 salt

1/4 ground black pepper

Olives to taste, chopped

2 whole-grain buns

Arugula leaves to taste

1 small cucumber

Directions

Prepare the hummus in first. Process the chickpeas in a blender.

Add the garlic and oil and blend well. Season with spices and add seeds.

Add the tahini and continue to blend for a few more minutes. Adjust the mixture with water.

Spread the hummus on both buns evenly, and layer the olives, arugula and cucumber.

Tex-Mex Vegan Migas

(Ready in about 25 minutes | Servings 4)

Ingredients

2 teaspoons olive oil

1 medium onion, peeled and diced

2 teaspoons garlic, minced

2 medium green bell pepper, diced

1 teaspoon turmeric

Chili Seasoning Mix

1 pound medium block Tofu, crumbled

1 ½ tablespoon nutritional yeast

1 small tomato, diced

1/2 teaspoon fresh coriander

1 tablespoon dark soy sauce

1/2 cup tortilla chip crumbs

Directions

Heat the olive oil in a saucepan or wok over medium heat. Sauté the onion, garlic, and peppers, stirring occasionally.

Cook until the onion is tender and translucent.

Stir in turmeric and Chili Seasoning Mix. Add the tofu into the vegetables.

Add the yeast, tomato, coriander and soy sauce and mix well.

Add tortillas and serve warm with a light salsa.

Whole-Wheat Crepes

(Ready in about 30 minutes | Servings 4)

Ingredients

1 cup whole-wheat flour

1 tablespoon potato starch

1/2 teaspoon sugar

1/2 teaspoon salt

2 tablespoons vegan margarine, melted

1/2 cup non-dairy milk

3/4 cup water

1 teaspoon vanilla

Nonstick cooking spray

Directions

Place all ingredients in an electric blender and mix well. Set the better aside for about 15 minutes.

Heat the frying-pan over medium heat. When the pan is hot, you can increase the heat to high. Coat the pan with nonstick cooking spray.

Quickly swirl the batter to distribute the mixture evenly over the pan. Fry the crepe until bubbles form on the top, about 3 minutes.

Carefully flip the crepe with a rubber spatula and cook the other side, until it is golden brown.

Serve hot, with maple syrup, marmalade, favorite dried fruits or vegan whipped cream.

Currant-Oat Scones

(Ready in about 35 minutes | Servings 8)

Ingredients

1 ½ cups all-purpose flour

1 cup oat bran

1 tablespoon baking powder

1 teaspoon baking soda

1/2 teaspoon salt

1/2 teaspoon brown sugar

1/4 teaspoon ground cinnamon

1/8 teaspoon ground nutmeg

1 cup currants

1/2 cup cold vegan margarine, cut into pieces

3/4 cup non-dairy milk

2 tablespoons rolled oats

Directions

Preheat the oven to 375 degrees F.

Mix the flour, oat bran, baking powder, baking soda, salt, sugar cinnamon, nutmeg and currants. Add margarine into the mixture, then add the milk. Mix until the dough holds together.

Transfer the dough on a floured surface and knead several times.

Roll the dough into a circle about 1 inch thick. Cut the circle into 8 squares or triangles. Transfer the scones on the prepared baking tray. Coat the scones with milk and sprinkle with the rolled oats.

Bake for 15 minutes, until risen and golden brown. Serve warm.

Apple Maple Sauce

(Ready in about 20 minutes | Servings 2)

Ingredients

1 apple

1/2 cup maple syrup

1/2 cup applesauce

1 teaspoon oil

2 teaspoon lemon juice

1/4 cup of water

1/4 cinnamon

2 tablespoons raisins

2 tablespoons walnuts, finaly chopped

Directions

Cut the apple into small chunks. Heat the oil in a saucepan over medium heat.

Add the apples in the pan and cook until they caramelize slightly.

Whisk the maple syrup with applesauce, lemon juice, water and cinnamon. Add to the pan and cook until the apples are crisp-tender.

Move from the stove and sprinkle with raisins and walnuts.

PART TWO LUNCH

Grandma's Vegetable Stock

(Ready in about 1 hour 45 minutes | Servings 4)

Ingredients

2 large red onions, cut into quarters

10 cloves garlic, minced

4 celery stalks, cut into small pieces

4 carrots, cut into halves lengthwise

2 parsnips, cut into small pieces

3 cups reserved vegetable trimmings

2 bay leaves

4-5 peppercorns

2 tablespoons parsley

2 sprigs fresh thyme

Directions

Place a soup pot on the stove on high heat. Put all ingredients in a large soup pot with 5 quarts of water. When the water is just about to boil, turn the heat to medium.

Simmer the stock for an hour. Taste the stock. If it seems weak, cook for about 30 minutes more. Turn off the heat.

Purée with an immersion blender. Strain the stock through a colander. Press on the vegetables in order to extract all the liquids.

Return the stock to the pot and reduce it to half its previous volume. Simmer over low heat to maintain the intense flavors.

Top with toasted pumpkin seeds. Ladle the soup into the small serving bowls.

Ginger Miso Soup with Tofu

(Ready in about 25 minutes | Servings 4)

Ingredients

4 cups water

1 cup button mushrooms, sliced

2 small onion, sliced

1 teaspoon garlic, minced

1 ½ teaspoons grated fresh ginger

1/2 cup carrots, sliced

1 3-inch piece of seaweed

1 cup green beans

2 bay leaves

4 tablespoons miso

8 to 10 ounces firm tofu, cut into small cubes

Directions

Put the water, mushrooms, onion, garlic, ginger, carrots, bay leaves and seaweed in a soup pot. Bring the soup to a boil over high heat.

Turn the heat to medium and simmer until the vegetables are soft. Add green beans. Simmer for 5 minutes.

In a small bowl, add 1 cup of the soup broth to the miso, and whisk slowly until miso is well dissolved. Add the tofu to the soup and whisk slowly. Serve hot.

Black-Eyed Peas with Herbs

(Ready in about 1 hour 20 minutes | Servings 4)

Ingredients

10 ounces dried blackeyed peas

1 red onion, finely chopped

1 parsnip, chopped

1 celery stalk, finely chopped

1/4 teaspoon paprika

2 tablespoons vegetable oil

1 teaspoon salt

1/2 teaspoon black pepper, ground

4-5 peppercorns

2 bay leaves

2 sprigs fresh thyme

1/2 teaspoon green chili paste, if desired

Directions

Preheat the skillet and saute the onion until it is soft. In a large pot add 4 cups of water, peas, parsnip, celery and bay leaves.

Turn the heat to medium and cook 30 minutes. Add herbs, paprika and chili (optional) and continue to cook for another 40 minutes.

Periodically check the peas and, if necessary, add additional water. Season with salt and pepper. Serve hot.

Juicy Spaghetti with Lentils

(Ready in about 1 hour 20 minutes | Servings 4)

Ingredients

1 cup brown lentils

1/2 teaspoon dried thyme

1 bunch fresh marjoram, finely chopped

2 cloves garlic, peeled and minced

2 cups tomato sauce

1 teaspoon white vinegar

1 onion, finely chopped

1 ½ teaspoons black pepper

1 teaspoon basil

1 teaspoon sea salt

8 ounces spaghetti

2 teaspoons olive oil

Directions

Heat a large saucepan. Put the lentils, thyme, marjoram, garlic and 2 cups of water in a saucepan and bring to boil over high heat.

Reduce heat, cook for 20 minutes, until lentils are al dente. Drain the lentils.

Combine the lentils with tomato sauce, vinegar, onion, pepper, basil, and salt. Cook over low heat for 30 minutes, stirring occasionally.

Cook the spaghetti. Drain and rinse. Transfer in a large serving bowl, drizzle the spaghetti with the olive oil.

Pour the lentil and tomato sauce over the spaghetti.

Full Flavor Mushroom Stock

(Ready in about 1 hour 25 minutes | Servings 4)

Ingredients

2 teaspoons olive oil

10 cauliflower florets

2 small onions, peeled and diced

2 cloves garlic, smashed

4 cups reserved mushroom stems

2 hearts of 1 bunch celery, cut into small pieces

1/2 ounce dried mushrooms

2 bay leaves

1 teaspoon fresh rosemary

1/3 teaspoon ground black pepper

Directions

Place a large soup pot on the stove on high heat. Pour the water in the pot and add all ingredients in a pot.

As soon as the water is boiling, turn the heat to medium.

Then simmer the stock for an hour or until all the vegetables are falling-apart tender.

Strain the stock through a colander. Press on the vegetables in order to extract all the excess liquids.

Return the stock to the soup pot and cook for 20 minutes more.

Szechuan Green Cabbage

(Ready in about 35 minutes | Servings 4)

Ingredients

1 small head green cabbage, cut into strips

2 tablespoons soy sauce

1 teaspoon olive oil

1 teaspoon sugar

2 teaspoons wine vinegar

2 tablespoons oil

1/4 teaspoon red pepper flakes

1 teaspoons grated ginger

1 teaspoon garlic, minced

Salt and pepper to taste

Directions

In a small bowl, whisk the soy sauce, olive oil, sugar and vinegar. Set aside.

Heat the oil in a wide saucepan over high heat. Add the red pepper flakes, ginger, and garlic, stirring constantly about 30 to 45 seconds.

Add the cabbage and cook for about 3 minutes. Combine with prepared sauce and mix well. Add salt and pepper.

Cook for 5 minutes longer and serve with chilies.

Spicy Hot Broccoli and Cauliflower

(Ready in about 35 minutes | Servings 4)

Ingredients

2 teaspoons vegetable oil

1 small hot chili

2 teaspoons grated fresh ginger

1/2 teaspoon chili powder

1/2 cayenne pepper

1/2 teaspoon coriander, ground

1/4 teaspoon salt

1/4 teaspoon black pepper

1 teaspoon basil

1 small head cauliflower, blanched

1 small head broccoli, blanched

1 teaspoon lemon juice

Togu (optional)

Directions

Heat the oil in a wide skillet or wok over medium heat. Add chili, ginger, chili powder, cayenne pepper, coriander, salt, pepper and basil.

Cut cauliflower and broccoli into florets.

Add 1/2 cup of water, cover and mix well. Let the vegetables steam for 4 minutes, until they are heated through. Add the lemon juice, garnish with tofu, decorate with lemon slices and serve warm.

Sweet Potato Soup

(Ready in about 1 hour | Servings 8)

Ingredients

8 cups water

1 teaspoon cumin seed

1 tablespoon vegetable oil

3 medium onions, diced

4 cloves garlic, minced

2 medium carrots, diced

3 pounds sweet potatoes, peeled, cut into small cubes

2 tablespoons lemon juice

Salt and pepper to taste

2 sprigs fresh thyme

Coriander to taste

Directions

Put cumin seeds in a soup pot and toast them over medium heat until tey are brown. Add the vegetable oil and turn the heat to medium-high.

Add the onions, garlic and carrots. Cook until the vegetables brown. Then add the thyme.

Add the sweet potatoes. Cook until the sweet potatoes are falling-apart tender or about 40 minutes.

Purée the soup and return it to the pot. Add the lemon juice and season with salt and pepper.

Top with coriander and serve hot.

Classic Pasta with Tomato Sauce

(Ready in about 30 minutes | Servings 4)

Ingredients

1 tablespoon oil

1 medium onion, chopped

2 cups tomatoes, chopped

1 clove garlic, minced

2 tablespoons tomato paste

1/2 teaspoon salt

1/8 black pepper

1/2 teaspoon sugar

1 cup water

2 tablespoons basil, chopped

1 teaspoon fresh rosemary

Directions

Heat the oil in a saucepan over medium heat. Saute the onion and garlic, until the garlic is soft and onion is translucent.

Add the tomato paste and cook, stirring occasionally. Add the tomatoes, salt, pepper, sugar and 1 cup of water.

Cook the sauce for about 20 minutes. Add the basil and rosemary.

Serve hot with favorite whole grain pasta.

Sunday Vegetable Lasagna

(Ready in about 1 hour 30 minutes | Servings 4)

Ingredients

1 large eggplant, sliced

2 large onions, sliced

1 medium green bell pepper, seeded and sliced

2 medium yellow bell pepper, seeded and sliced

2 tablespoons olive oil

2 medium zucchini, sliced

6 tomatoes, cut into halves

3 cups Tomato Sauce

2 tablespoon fresh basil, chopped

1 teaspoon oregano

3 large pasta sheets

Directions

Sprinkle salt on the both sides of the eggplant slices and place in a large bowl. After 30 minutes transfer them in a colander to drain. Rinse eggplant slices and dry them.

Meanwhile, preheat a grill plate to high temperature.

Prepare baking tray and line with parchment. Layer the eggplant, onions, and peppers in a single layer on a baking tray. Brush with oil each piece. Broil them for 3 minutes on each side. Then broil the zucchini and tomatoes until they are crisp and soft.

Reduce the temperature to 350 degrees F. Combine the herbs in a small bowl.

Grease a large baking dish. Spread tomato sauce over the bottom of the dish. Top the sauce with one sheet of pasta. Sprinkle with one-fourth the herb mixture and then spread with tomato sauce. Layer half of the vegetables on the pasta sheet. Sprinkle them with another fourth of the herb mixture. Layer the pasta sheet. Sprinkle another fourth of the herb mixture.

Layer the rest of the vegetables on the pasta sheet. Top with the remaining herbs again. Layer the last pasta sheet on top. Spread the last cup of tomato sauce on top of the third pasta sheet.

Cover the lasagna with aluminium foil. Bake for 35 minutes.

Festive Barley Pilaf

(Ready in about 1 hour | Servings 4)

Ingredients

1 cup barley

3 tablespoons vegetable oil

1 medium onion, diced

2 cloves garlic, minced

2 medium carrots, cut into matchsticks

2 teaspoons fresh ginger, grated

1 cup blanched English peas

2 teaspoons soy sauce

1/4 cup toasted pine nuts

1/2 teaspoon salt

1/8 black pepper

1/8 red pepper flakes

Directions

Heat a large saucepan over medium heat. Add the barley and cook until it begins to brown. Transfer barley in a bowl and set aside.

Heat 2 tablespoons of the oil in the saucepan, and sauté the onion, garlic, carrots, and ginger until the onion is translucent. Add the barley and cook for another 4 minutes.

Then add 3 cups of water, cover, and simmer for about 20 minutes. Add the blanched peas, soy sauce and pine nuts.

Stir in 1 tablespoon oil and season with salt, pepper and pepper flakes. Cook for 10 minutes longer and serve warm.

Lazy Day Baked Rice

(Ready in about 1 hour 30 minutes | Servings 4)

Ingredients

2 cups brown rice

2 canola oil

2 ½ cups Vegetable Stock

1 teaspoon salt

1/4 ground black pepper

Parsley (optional

Directions

Preheat the oven to 350 degrees F.

Rinse the rice in 5 to 8 changes of water until the water is clear. Drain washed rice.

Heat the oil in a skillet. Sauté the rice for about 5 minutes. Add Vegetable Stock, salt and black pepper to the rice. Transfer the rice to a baking dish and place in the oven.

Cook the rice for 30 minutes, until the water is well absorbed. Sprinkle with parsley and serve warm.

Multi-Bean Chili with Herbs

(Ready in about 1 hour 30 minutes | Servings 4)

Ingredients

1/4 cup dried chickpeas

1/4 cup dried Great Northern beans

1/4 cup dried soybeans

1/4 cup dried kidney beans

1/4 cup dried cranberry beans

1/4 cup dried black turtle beans

2 teaspoons oil

1 medium onion, diced

1 teaspoon minced garlic

1 teaspoon dried oregano

2 bay leaves

1 stalk celery, diced

2 medium red bell pepper, diced

1 teaspoon chili powder

1/4 teaspoon black pepper and 4-5 peppercorns

1 teaspoon ground cumin

1/2 teaspoon ground coriander

1 cup tomatoes, diced

1/4 cup black vinegar

1 teaspoon salt

Directions

Rinse and soak the beans. Put the beans in a large pot with 8 cups of the water, oregano, and bay leaves. Bring the beans to a boil, reduce the heat to medium, and simmer for 2 hours in a slow cooker.

Check the beans periodically and add more water if it is necessary. Cook until the beans are tender.

Meanwhile, heat the oil in a saucepan over medium heat and sauté the onion, garlic, oregano, celery, peppers, chili powder, cumin, and coriander for 6 minutes.

Stir in the tomatoes and vinegar and mix well. Continue cooking, until all ingredients are soft. Add the mixture to the beans.

Cook for another 30 minutes. Season with salt and pepper and serve hot.

Cheap Curied Rice

(Ready in about 1 hour 30 minutes | Servings 4)

Ingredients

2 cups basmati rice

2 tablespoon groundnut, chopped

1 onion, finely chopped

3 cloves garlic, minced

3 tablespoons oil

4 teaspoons sweet curry

2 teaspoons salt

1/4 teaspoon blach ground pepper

1/8 teaspoon tumeric

1/8 teaspoon cumin

3 ½ sups Water

Lemon slices (optional)

Directions

Sauté onions and garlic in the preheated oil in a heavy saucepan over medium heat, until the onion is soft. Add rice and curry and cook, stirring frequently, about 1 to 2 minutes.

Add water, salt, pepper, tumeric and cumin, and bring to a boil, until the rice on top appears dry.

Reduce the heat to low and cover, continue to cook another 15 minutes.

Remove saucepan from heat, sprinkle with groundnut, adjust seasonings to taste and decorate with lemon slices.

Farfalle with Portobellos

(Ready in about 30 minutes | Servings 2)

Ingredients

8 ounces farfalle	1/2 cup water
2 teaspoons extra-virgin olive oil	1/2 teaspoon salt
1 medium onion, peeled and sliced	1/2 teaspoon ground black pepper
3 cloves garlic, minced	Basil to taste
2 portobello mushrooms, sliced on strips	1 teaspoon fresh thyme
1 cup Sun-Dried Tomato Pesto	1/2 cup Tofu Parmesan, grated

Directions

Cook the farfalle according to the directions on a package. Transfer to a colander, drain and rinse. Put the farfalle in a serving bowl and set aside.

Heat the oil in a saucepan over medium heat. Sauté the onion and garlic in a saucepan, until the onion is tender.

Add the portobellos and cook about 4 minutes, stirring slowly. Add the pesto and water to the pan. Add the farfalle and mix well. Season farfalle and sprinkle with basil and thyme.

Sprinkle parmesan on the top and serve warm.

Vegetable Risotto

(Ready in about 30 minutes | Servings 4)

Ingredients

2 cups long-grain white rice

6 cups Vegetable Stock

2 tablespoons sesame oil

1 leeks, sliced

3 cloves garlic

1 ½ teaspoon dried basil

1/2 cup white wine

1 medium zucchini, sliced

2 medium red bell pepper, seeded and sliced

2 carrots, sliced

2 tablespoon lemon zest

1/4 cup extra virgin olive oil

1/4 cup tomatoes, diced

Salt and pepper to taste

2 sprigs of thyme

Directions

Heat the oil in a wide skillet over medium heat and sauté the rice, leeks, garlic and basil. Cook, until the rice begins to brown. Add the wine and cook, stirring frequently, until the rice absorbs the wine.

In a large soup pot, heat the stock over low heat and add 1 cup of the stock to the prepared rice. Continue cooking, until most of the stock is absorbed.

Add the zucchini, red bell pepper and carrots. Continue adding the stock, 1 cup at a time, and cook until the most of the stock is absorbed.

When the vegetables are just soft, remove the pot from the heat. Add salt and pepper.

Stir in the lemon, 3 tablespoons of the olive oil, tomatoes, and thyme. Taste for seasoning. Combine vegetables with the rice mixture, stirring gently. Serve warm.

Macaroni and Tofu Cheese

(Ready in about 35 minutes | Servings 6)

Ingredients

1/2 cup whole wheat flour

1/4 cup nutritional yeast

1 clove garlic, minced

1/4 teaspoon cayenne pepper

1/4 cup vegan margarine

1/2 teaspoon dried mustard

4 cups cooked macaroni

½ cup firm tofu, grated

1 tablespoon mayonnaise

Salt and pepper to taste

1/2 teaspoon oregano

Directions

Toast the flour and yeast in a saucepan over low-medium heat, until they begin to take on some color. Carefully whisk 2 cups of water into the flour mixture, making sure that there are no lumps form. Add garlic and cayenne pepper and mix well.

Cook the mixture about 8 to 10 minutes. Add the margarine and mustard and stir well. Season the mixture and stir in the macaroni.

Top with tofu and mayonnaise. Serve warm.

Pilaf with Cashews and Tomatoes

(Ready in about 1 hour | Servings 2)

Ingredients

1 tablespoons olive oil

1 tablespoons sesame oil

1/4 cup leeks, chopped

2 cloves minced garlic

1/2 cup toasted cashews, finely chopped

1 cup coarse bulgur, rinsed

1 teaspoon sea salt

1/4 teaspoon black pepper

5 Tomatoes, sliced

2 tablespoons fresh cinnamon basil, chopped

fresh chopped parsley (optional)

Directions

Heat the oil in a wide saucepan or wok over medium heat. Sauté the leeks, garlic, and half of the cashews until the onions are just tender.

Preheat the oven to 375 degrees F. Transfer the onion mixture to a medium ovenproof casserole dish. Add the bulgur, 2 cups of the hot water, salt, pepper, and tomatoes. Cover the casserole and bake for 30 minutes.

Remove the pilaf from the oven, stir in the basil, and let stand to allow the bulgur to steam for 20 minutes.

Sprinkle the pilaf with the another half of cashews and fresh chopped parsley.

Couscous with Berries and Nuts

(Ready in about 30 minutes | Servings 4)

Ingredients

1/4 cup dried berries (e.g. blueberries, cranberries, raisins)

3 tablespoons walnuts

2 teaspoons extra-virgin olive oil

1 medium red onion, finely chopped

1/2 teaspoon fresh thyme

1/2 teaspoon fresh basil

Salt and pepper to taste

1/2 teaspoon paprika

2 cups cooked couscous

Directions

Cover the berries with a hot water in a small bowl, and let the berries stand for 15 minutes.

Heat a saucepan over medium heat. Add the walnuts and cook, until the nuts begin to take on some brown color. Turn off heat and set walnuts aside.

Heat the oil in a saucepan, and then sauté the onion until it is soft. Add the thyme, basil, paprika, couscous, and mix well.

Season your meal and add berries and walnuts to the couscous. Serve warm.

Spiced Veggie Couscous

(Ready in about 35 minutes | Servings 4)

Ingredients

2 cups cooked couscous

2 tablespoon vegetable oil

1 medium yellow onion, diced

2 cloves garlic, minced

1 teaspoon curry powder

1/2 teaspoon ground cumin

1/2 teaspoon ground ginger

2 carrots, finely diced

1 small green bell pepper, seeded and sliced

1 tomato, chopped

Directions

In a wok or wide saucepan, heat 1 tablespoon of the vegetable oil. Sauté the onion and garlic, until the onion begins to soft. Add the dry spices and mix well.

The mixture is thick now. Cook the mixture for 10 minutes. Add the couscous to the wok and mix well. Remove the couscous to a bowl.

Heat the remaining tablespoon of the oil over medium heat and sauté the carrots for 2 minutes. Add the peppers and sauté for 2 minutes more.

Combine the mixture with the couscous. Serve hot.

Tricolor Rice Pilaf

(Ready in about 45 minutes | Servings 4)

Ingredients

2 cups cooked basmati rice

2 tablespoon canola oil

1 small onion red, chopped

1 teaspon garlic, minced

1 zucchini, sliced

1 carrots, cut into matchsticks

1/4 cup sliced cashews

1 teaspoon sea salt

1/4 teaspoon black pepper, ground

1 ½ cups non-diary milk

1 ¼ cups water

Parsley (optional)

Directions

Preheat the oven to 375 degrees F.

Rinse the rice in several changes of water and drain them.

Heat the oil in a wide skillet over medium heat. Sauté the onion and garlic until the onion begins to soft.

Add the zucchini, carrots and cook for 5 minutes, until all the vegetables are soft. Add cashews, salt and pepper. Add the washed rice, milk and water.

Bring to a boil and transfer in the oven. Bake for 25 minutes.

Leave to steam and toss the remaining cashews and parsley.

Grilled Asparagus with Cashews

(Ready in about 35 minutes | Servings 2)

Ingredients

1 pound asparagus, blanched

2 large onion, peeled

1 tablespoon extra-virgin olive oil

Salt and pepper

1 teaspoon fresh thyme

1/4 cup French Vinaigrette

1/4 cup sliced Cashews, toasted

Directions

In a wide saucepan or wok, cook the onions in salted water until they are tender. Rinse and drain. Cut the onions into halves lengthwise.

Drizzle the asparagus and onions with the oil and add salt and pepper. Preheat grill.

Grill the onions over high heat for 3 minutes, then turn them and grill the other side. Grill the asparagus over high heat to desired tenderness.

Drizzle the vegetables with vinaigrette and sprinkle with thyme and cashews. Serve hot.

Fennel with Onions and Tomatoes

(Ready in about 50 minutes | Servings 2)

Ingredients

1 tablespoon oil

2 fennel bulbs, cut into halves

2 small onions, sliced

salt and ground black pepper to taste

1/3 cup white wine

8 cloves garlic, peeled

1/4 cup kalamata olives, quartered

1 cup fresh tomatoes, diced

1 teaspoon oregano

Directions

Preheat the oven to 400 degrees F. Coat your baking dich with a very small amount of the oil.

Heat the oil in a large saucepan over medium heat.

Carefully add the fennel and onions. Cook until the vegetables begin to brown, or about 3 minutes. Turn on the other side and cook for another 3 minutes.

Layer the onions and fennel to the baking dish. Season with the salt and black pepper. Add the wine, garlic and olives to the baking dish.

Cover the dish with aluminium foil and bake for 30 minutes, or until the fennel is soft and just crisped.

Add the tomatoes to the baking dish and bake for another 5 minutes. Sprinkle with oregano and serve warm.

Spicy Green Beans

(Ready in about 50 minutes | Servings 4)

Ingredients

1 pound green beans	2 bay leaves
2 tablespoon oil	A pinch of sea salt
1 large red onion, chopped	1/8 teaspoon black pepper
2 cloves garlic minced	1/2 teaspoon paprika
1 red bell pepper, seeded and sliced	5-6 peppercorns

Directions

Cook the green beans for about 30 minutes, or until the beans are tender, but they are not overcooked. Heat the oil in an iron-skillet over medium heat. Saute the onion and garlic, until the onion is soft and translucent.

Season with salt and pepper, add bell pepper, bay leaves and add 1/4 cup of the water to the skillet. Cook until the pepper is soft.

Add the green beans, paprika, peppercorns and mix carefully. Serve warm.

Christmas Cabbage Rolls

(Ready in about 1 hour 30 minutes | Servings 10)

Ingredients

1 cup canned chickpeas, rinsed and drained

1 cup cooked brown rice

1 cup oat bran

1/2 teaspoon marjoram

1 medium onion

2 tablespoons soy sauce

1 tablespoon mustard

20 large cabbage leaves

1 cup tomato juice

1/2 teaspoon Kosher Salt

1/8 teaspoon ground black pepper

5 peppercorns

1/4 teaspoon paprika

1 tablespoon dry minced parsley

Directions

Preheat the oven to 350 degrees F.

Combine the chickpeas and brown rice and blend with a food processor until the mixture forms a mash. Divide the mixture into ten equal pieces.

In the large mixing bowl, combine mash with the oat bran, marjoram, onion, soy sauce and mustard. Add salt and pepper and set aside.

Bring a stockpot of water to a boil. Add the cabbage leaves and cook for 3 minutes. Drain the leaves thoroughly.

Place a cabbage leaf on your work surface. Place 1/10 of filling on each cabbage leaf. Place the filling at one edge of the cabbage leaf. Beginning from the cut end of the leaf, and roll it up, folding in the edges as you go.

Place the cabbage rolls, side-by-side in a baking dish. Sprinkle with peppercorns.

Pour tomato juice over the rolls. Add paprika and parsley. Adjust seasonings. Bake the cabbage rolls for 45 to 50 minutes, until they are brown.

Hungarian Vegan Paprikás

(Ready in about 50 minutes | Servings 4)

Ingredients

2 tablespoons oil	1 medium tomato, diced
1 medium onion, diced	1 tablespoon paprika
2 cloves garlic, crushed	1 teaspoon cayenne pepper
1 pound seitan, drained	1/2 teaspoon salt
1 red bell pepper, chopped	1/4 black pepper
1 green bell pepper, chopped	1/2 cup Tofu

Directions

Heat the oil in a skillet over medium-high heat. Sauté the onion and garlic, until the onion is translucent.

Add the seitan, peppers, tomato, paprika, cayenne pepper and 1/2 cup water. Bring to a boil.

Lower the heat, and simmer for 15 minutes.

Add salt and pepper. Serve hot with tofu cheese.

Rice Noodles with Tofu

(Ready in about 30 minutes | Servings 2)

Ingredients

3 tablespoons soy sauce

2 tablespoons lime juice

2 teaspoons sesame oil

1 cup firm tofu, cut into bite-size pieces

1 cup flat rice stick noodles

2 tablespoons olive oil

2 cloves garlic, minced

1 yellow bell pepper, diced

1 cup snow peas

1 cup whole baby corn, drained and rinsed

Directions

Prepare the marinade in first. Mix the soy sauce, lime juice and sesame oil in a mixing bowl. Pour the marinade over the tofu and set aside.

Bring a large stockpot of water to a boil. Remove from heat and add the noodles to the hot water. Soak the noodles, until the noodles are al dente.

Drain the noodles and rinse under cold water. Set aside.

Heat the olive oil in a wide saucepan or wok over medium-high heat. Add the garlic and cook, for 1-2 minutes. Add the bell pepper, snow peas, baby corn, and stir-fry for 2 to 3 minutes.

Add the noodles and tofu to the saucepan and cook, stirring occasionally, until the noodles are warmed through.

Party Veggie Burgers

(Ready in about 1 hour | Servings 6)

Ingredients

2 cups cooked lentils

1/2 cup dry amaranth

1 tablespoon canola oil

1/2 cup onion, finely diced

2 cloves garlic, minced

1 large carrot, peeled and grated

1/2 cup instant oats

2 tablespoons tomato pasta sauce

2 tablespoons nutritional yeast flakes

salt, or to taste

ground black pepper to taste

Directions

Drain the cooked lentils and add to the mixing bowl.

Bring a pot of water to boil Add the amaranth. Reduce the heat to low temperature, cover and simmer about 25 minutes. Add the cooked amaranth to the lentils.

Preheat the oven to 350 degrees F. Line a baking tray with parchment paper.

Heat the oil in a cast-iron skillet over medium heat. Sauté the onion, garlic, carrots, until the carrots are tender. Add to the mixing bowl. Then add along with the oats, tomato pasta sauce, yeast, salt and pepper.

Shape mixture into 12 to 13 small patties with your fingers and transfer them on the prepared baking tray.

Bake for 20 minutes, until dry on the top, then turn the patties over and bake for another 10 minutes, until they are dark brown.

Serve with whole-grain buns, mustard, ketchup, vegan mayonnaise and your favorite salad.

Quick Ginger Curry

(Ready in about 20 minutes | Servings 4)

Ingredients

1 tablespoon canola oil

1 onion, peeled and sliced

2 garlic cloves, minced

1 tablespoon grated fresh ginger

1 cup chopped cauliflower florets

1 cup chopped broccoli florets

2 teaspoons curry paste

Sea salt to taste

1 (14 oz) can non-diary milk

2 tablespoons fresh parsley

1 tablespoon fresh thyme

Directions

Heat the oil in a large iron-skillet over medium heat. Sauté the onions, garlic and ginger until the onion is tender.

Add cauliflower and broccoli, and cook until they are soft. Sir in the curry paste and non-diary milk and simmer for about 5 more minutes.

Season with salt and pepper. Sprinkle with chopped almonds, parsley and thyme, and serve hot.

Edamame and Rice Bowl

(Ready in about 40 minutes | Servings 4)

Ingredients

1/4 cup wakame seaweed

1 tablespoon soy sauce

2 teaspoons sesame oil

1 tablespoon apple vinegar

2 tablespoons vegetable oil

2 cups cooked brown rice

1/2 teaspoon minced garlic

1 medium carrot, sliced

4 leeks, sliced

1/2 cup edamame

Salt and black pepper to taste

Directions

Cover the wakame with boiling water in a small bowl. Let the wakame seaweed soaks for 10 minutes. Drain and set aside.

Mix the soy sauce, sesame oil, vinegar and vegetable oil in a mixing bowl.

Combine the rice, garlic, carrot, leeks, edamame and wakame seaweed with soy sauce mixture.

Let stand 20 minutes and serve.

Tempeh and Tomato with Rice

(Ready in about 30 minutes | Servings 2)

Ingredients

1 tablespoon grapeseed oil

1/4 teaspoon mustard seeds

1 large onion, sliced

1/2 teaspoon chili powder

1 cup tomatoes, sliced

1/2 teaspoon salt

1 8-ounce package tempeh, sliced

1 cup cooked brown rice

2 teaspoons basil

1/2 rosemary

Directions

Heat the oil in a large saucepan over medium heat. Add the mustard seeds. When the mustard seeds start to pop, add the chili and onion.

Cook about 10 minutes. Add the tomatoes, salt, and tempeh. Cook another 15 minutes.

Sprinkle with basil and rosemary and serve over rice.

Noodles in Almond Sauce

(Ready in about 30 minutes | Servings 2)

Ingredients

1 tablespoon canola oil

1 yellow onion, sliced

2 cloves garlic, crush

1/2 pound dry noodles

1/4 teaspoon paprika

1 cup broccoli florets

1 cup Vegan Almond Sauce

2 tablespoons almonds, toasted and chopped

1 tablespoon lemon juice

Hot peppers to taste

vegan sour cream, if desured

Directions

Bring a large stockpot of the water to a boil. Add the noodles, turn the heat to medium and cook until the noodles are al dente and chewy. Drain and rinse. Reserve.

Heat the oil in a wide iron-skillet and saute the onion and garlic, until the onion starts to develop translucent color. Add paprika and broccoli. Stir-fry until the vegetables are crisp-tender.

Add the vegan almond sauce and lemon. Stir in the noodles. Toss the chopped almonds into prepared meal. Garnish with 2 hot peppers and 1 tablespoon vegan sour cream.

Spiced Eggplant with Roasted Polenta

(Ready in about 1 hours | Servings 2)

Ingredients

2 medium eggplants	1/2 teaspoon sea salt
1/4 cup roasted polenta	1/4 teaspoon ground black pepper
1 teaspoon garlic powder	1 teaspoon fresh basil
2 tablespoons canola oil	2 cups tomato sauce
1/2 cup roasted red peppers	Vegan sour cream (optional)
1 teaspoon dry oregano	

Directions

Preheat the oven to 350 degrees F. Sprinkle non-stick spray to coat a baking tray.

Cut the eggplant lengthwise into long slices. Add salt to the slices and place them in a colander for 30 minutes. Drain salted eggplant and rinse it with cold clean water.

Sprinkle each slice with oil and roast until they are soft. Season with salt and pepper.

Cut the polenta into pieces.

Then make the eggplant rolls. Add garlic powder, red pepper, oregano, basil and polenta at the narrow end of the eggplant. Roll eggplant slices to enclose the filling.

Repeat procedure with eash eggplant slice. Pour the tomato sauce in the baking tray. Adjust the seasonings. Transfer rolls to the baking tray

Bake for 20 minutes, until the rolls are heated through and garnish your meal with vegan sour cream.

Spring Peas with Mayonnaise and Mustard

(Ready in about 30 minutes | Servings 4)

Ingredients

1 pound green peas, blanched

1 tablespoon canola oil

2 spreeng leeks, chopped

2 small carrots, sliced

2 cloves garlic, 2 teaspoon minced

1 teaspoon dry dill

2 tablespoons grainy mustard

A dash of salt and pepper

2 tablespoons eggless mayonnaise

Directions

Reheat the green peas and keep warm.

Heat the oil in a wide sauce or wok over medium-high heat. Add the leeks and garlic and sauté until the onion is translucent, or about 3 minutes.

Add the carrots, mustard and dill, and season with salt and pepper. Add 1/4 cup of water to the saucepan and bring it to boil. Simmer for a few minutes, until the carrots begin to tender.

Stir in the green peas. Mix gently and serve with vegan eggless mayonnaise.

Noodles and Tofu in a Soy Sauce

(Ready in about 45 minutes | Servings 2)

Ingredients

3 tablespoons soy sauce

1 tablespoon sherry

1 tablespoon hoisin sauce

1/2 cup dry rice noodles

3 teaspoons canola oil

1 onion, peeled sliced

1 teaspoon garlic, minced

1 carrot, sliced

6 mushrooms, sliced

1 teaspoon ginger, grated

1/2 cup cauliflower florets

1/2 cup baked tofu cut into strips

1 parsnip, cut into thin slices

1 teaspoon sesame oil

Salt and pepper to taste

2 leeks, finaly chopped

2 tablespoons chopped fresh basil

Directions

Mix the soy sauces, sherry and hoisin sauce in a mixing bowl. Set aside.

Bring a large stockpot of salted water to the boiling point, and cook noodles for 5 minutes. Drain and rinse the noodles. Set aside.

Heat the oil in a wok or large wide saucepan over medium-high flame. Add the noodles and stir-fry for 3. Transfer the noodles to a serving platter.

Heat the saucepan again and add another teaspoon of the oil. Add the onion, garlic, carrots, mushrooms and ginger, cook until the onion is tender.

Add the cauliflower florets, tofu, and parsnip and cook until the vegetables are soft and crispy. Add the prepared sauce, sesame oil, season with salt and pepper, stirring carefully.

Add the noodles and stir to mix all ingredients well. Then cook until the noodles are heated through. Sprinkle with leeks and basil and serve warm.

Veggie Summer Day

(Ready in about 40 minutes | Servings 4)

Ingredients

1 ½ cups bean sprouts, cooked	2 tablespoon tomato juice
2 tablespoons vegetable oil	1/2 teaspoon salt
1 medium red onions, peeled and chopped	¼ teaspoon pepper
2 cloves garlic, minced	1 teaspoon dill
1 large carrots, sliced	2 bay leaves
1 small parsnip, sliced	2 tablespoons non-diary sour cream.
1 small tomato, chopped	

Directions

Blanch the bean sprouts, set aside and keep warm.

Heat the oil in a wide skillet over high-medium flame. Sauté the onion and garlic, till the onion is tender or 2 minutes. Add carrots, parsnip, tomato pieces, bay leaves and 1/2 cup of water to the saucepan and bring it to boil.

Stir in tomato juice, season with salt, pepper and dill, and simmer for about 10 minutes.

Garnish with sour cream and serve hot.

Light Spring Salad

(Ready in about 20 minutes | Servings 2)

Ingredients

2 cloves garlic, crushed

1/8 teaspoon cayenne pepper

1/2 teaspoon coriander, ground

2 tablespoons lemon juice

3 tablespoons extra-virgin olive oil

4 carrots, cut into matchsticks

Salt and pepper

1 head lettuce, washed and trimmed

8 cherry tomatoes, cut into halves.

1 large cucumber, cut into matchsticks

1 teaspoon cumin.

Directions

Mix the garlic, seasonings, lemon juice, and olive oil in a medium mixing bowl.

Add the carrots, and let stand for the flavors to develop. Adjust seasonings.

Season with salt and pepper. Remove to a serving platter.

Arrange the lettuce, tomatoes and cucumber along the salads. Sprinkle with cumin. Serve cool with your favorite vegan meal.

Hot and Spicy Cooked Corn

(Ready in about 20 minutes | Servings 2)

Ingredients

2 ears corn, shucked and cut into 3-inch lengths

1 tablespoon oil

1 medium onion, sliced

2 cloves garlic, minced

1/4 teaspoon red pepper flakes

1/4 teaspoon paprika

1 teaspoon sea salt

1/4 black pepper

Lemon halves (optional)

Directions

Bring a large stockpot of water to a boil, add prepared corn, and cook for 5 minutes, unil the kernels are soft.

During this time, heat the oil in a wide iron-skillet over medium-high flame. Then cook the onion, garlic, and pepper and paprika until the onion is tender.

Remove the corn from the stockpot. Put the corn in the iron-skillet. Cook the corn until it begins to brown. Sprinkle with salt and pepper and adjust seasonings.

Sprinkle with additional red pepper flakes, if desired, and garnish with lemon halves.

Bean Sprouts with Roasted Tofu Cubes

(Ready in about 1 hour | Servings 6)

Ingredients

1 cup bean sprouts, cooked

3 cups long-grain rice, cooked

1 cup yellow onions, peeled and chopped

2 cloves garlic, minced

2 tablespoons vegetable oil

1/2 teaspoon salt

¼ teaspoon pepper

1 teaspoon fresh basil

1 cup roasted tofu, cut into small cubes

Directions

Heat the oil in a wide saucepan over a high heat. Add onions and garlic, and cook until the onions are translucent and soft. Season with spices.

Drain and rinse bean sprouts. Add the cooked rice and basil. Mix all ingredients well. Reserve.

Meanwhile, preheat the oven to 350 degrees F. Line a medium baking sheet with parchment.

Place the tofu on the baking sheet and bake for about 30 minutes, or till the tofu cubes are lightly golden-brown.

Garnish with roasted tofu cubes and serve warm.

Macaroni in Green-Red Sauce

(Ready in about 35 minutes | Servings 4)

Ingredients

1 package macaroni (per 4 servings)

1 ½ tablespoons oil

3 spring leeks, sliced

3 cloves garlic, minced

1⁄4 cup dry white wine

4 tomatoes, chopped

1 teaspoon fresh rosemary

1/2 teaspoon paprika

1 teaspoon oregano

1/2 sea salt

1/4 black pepper

Directions

Heat the oil in a wide saucepan over high-medium flame. Sauté the leeks the garlic till the leeks are soft-crispy.

Add the wine to the saucepan and simmer until all liquid is almost evaporated.

Add the tomatoes, rosemary, paprika and oregano, and cook until the tomatoes are warmed through. Season the sauce with salt and pepper.

Cook the macaroni according to instructions on a package. Pour the green-red sauce over macaroni and serve warm.

Corn with Shiitakes

(Ready in about 30 minutes | Servings 4)

Ingredients

2 teaspoons canola oil

1 medium onion, sliced

2 teaspoons garlic, minced

1 cup shiitake mushrooms, sliced

2 medium green bell pepper, seeded and sliced

2 cups corn kernels

1 teaspoon basil

Salt and pepper

Croutons (optional)

Directions

Heat the canola oil in a wide saucepan or wok over medium flame. Sauté the onions and garlic until the onion is tender and translucent, or about 2 minutes.

Add the shiitakes and peppers and cook for 3 minutes more. Then, add the corn kernels.

Reduce the heat to low, and simmer your dish for 5 minutes longer.

Stir in the basil and garnish with your favorite Croutons.

Oyster Mushrooms with Roasted Tofu Cubes

(Ready in about 40 minutes | Servings 4)

Ingredients

1 cup Oyster mushrooms

1 tablespoon extra-virgin olive oil

1 large red onion

2 cloves garlic

1 red bell pepper, seeded and sliced

1 teaspoon dry oregano

1 sprig fresh thyme

1/2 teaspoon dry basil

1 cup roasted tofu

Directions

Heat the saucepan over high heat. Heat the oil and sauté onion and garlic, until the onion is translucent and soft, or for 10 minutes.

Reduce the heat to law and add mushrooms. Season mushrooms with salt and pepper. Add bell peppers.

Stir-fry for another 5 minutes, stirring occasionally to prevent mushrooms to burn and stick to the bottom of the saucepan.

Add oregano, thyme and basil and continue to cook for another 5 minutes. Remove from the heat and reserve.

Meanwhile, prepare tofu cubes. Preheat the oven to 350 degrees F. Line a medium baking sheet with parchment.

Layer the tofu on the baking sheet and bake for about 30 minutes. Bake till tofu cubes begin to develop gold color.

Garnish Oyster mushrooms with tofu and serve immediately.

Quick Garden Peas

(Ready in about 30 minutes | Servings 2)

Ingredients

1 teaspoon oil

1 small leek, sliced

1/2 teaspoon minced garlic

2 tablespoons lime juice

1 cup fresh garden peas

1/4 teaspoon tarragon

1/2 cup tomatoes, chopped

2 teaspoons fresh dill, chopped

Sea salt to taste

black pepper to taste

1 teaspoon parsley

Directions

Heat a wide iron-skillet over medium-low heat and add the oil. When the oil begins to smoke, add the leeks and garlic.

Cook till the leeks are tender or for 3 to 4 minutes. Raise the heat and add the lime juice.

When the liquid is mostly evaporated, add the garden peas amd tarragon.

Then reduce the heat to medium, and cook until the peas are soft but not overcooked, for 5 minutes. Season with salt and pepper.

Add chopped tomato and dill, mix well and cover the pan. Cook for another 10 minutes, taste and adjust seasonings.

Toss with parsley and serve hot.

Curry Potatoes with Mayonnaise

(Ready in about 40 minutes | Servings 4)

Ingredients

1 pound potatoes, peeled,	1/2 teaspoon mustard
1 tablespoon grapeseed oil	1 teaspoon coriander powder
2 onions, finaly chopped	1 sprig curry leaves
2 chilies, chopped	1/2 teaspoon sea salt
2 tomatoes, chopped	2 tablespoons eggless mayonnaise
1/2 cup water	Parsley (optional)

Directions

Cook the potatoes for 30 minutes. Drain, rinse and cut them into small pieces. Set aside.

Meanwhile, heat the grapeseed oil in a wide saucepan.

When the oil starts to smoke, add onions and chilies, and sauté for 5 minutes.

Then add the tomatoes and cook until they are soft. Then add boiled potatoes and mix gently.

Add 1/2 cup water, add curry, salt and mustard and cook until the liquid evaporates.

Add coriander powder.

Remove from heat. Sprinkle with parsley and garnish with mayonnaise.

Red Spicy Potatoes with Cauliflower

(Ready in about 40 minutes | Servings 4)

Ingredients

1 medium head cauliflower, cut into florets

4 medium potatoes, peeled and cubed

1/4 cup vegetable oil

1 teaspoon cumin seeds

1/2 teaspoon turmeric powder

1/2 teaspoon paprika

1/2 teaspoon cayenne pepper

1/2 cup tomato paste, fresh or canned

1 teaspoon garam masala

2 teaspoon coriander powder

1/2 teaspoon kosher salt

Directions

Heat the oil in a large saucepan, then saute cumin seeds for 1 minute. Cut potatoes into small bite sized cubes and add to a saucepan.

Then add turmeric, paprika and cayenne. Cook for few minutes, or till the spices begin to brown.

In a saucepan combine tomato paste, garam masala and coriander, and simmer for 5 to 6 minutes. Continue stirring the sauce and season with kosher salt and adjust the seasonings.

Add cauliflower florets, raise the heat and cook for 5 minutes more.

Lower the heat, cover and simmer for about 15 minutes until the sauce becomes dry.

Broccoli with Soy Sausages

(Ready in about 30 minutes | Servings 4)

Ingredients

2 cups broccoli

1/4 cup vegan margarine

1" ginger piece, grated

1/2 teaspoon sea salt

1/4 fresh ground pepper

1/4 red pepper flakes

4 soy sausages

2 teaspoons mustard

Directions

Break up the broccoli into florets. Cut the ginger into very small pieces. Bring a large stock pan of salted water to the boil and add broccoli and ginger.

Heat margarine in a wok or heavy pan, and add broccoli. Add water to the pan, and continue to cook for about 20 minutes or until broccoli is tender.

Add salt, pepper, red pepper and stir well.

Prepare sausages acording to package instructions. Cut the sausages into bite-sized slices. Place over broccoli, garnish with mustard and serve warm.

Indian Spinach with spicy Potatoes

(Ready in about 40 minutes | Servings 2)

Ingredients

2 cups fresh spinach, washed

3 cloves garlic, minced

1 bay leaf

2 onions, chopped

1/2 cup potatoes, washed and peeled

1 teaspoon turmeric

3 tablespoons oil

1teaspoon garam masala

1 teaspoon cumin powder

Salt to taste

Fresh ground black pepper

4 tablespoons vegan sour cream

Directions

Boil the spinach with garlic and bay leaf. Process them in an electric blender to a fine puree. Reserve.

Cut potatoes into bite-sized cubes and cook with salt and turmeric in a large pot, for about 15 minutes or till the potatoes are soft but not overcooked.

Heat the oil in a heavy fry pan and fry onions with spinach puree (or paste) and cook for another few minutes.

Add the boiled potatoes, garam masala, cumin powder, salt and black pepper to taste. Cook for few minutes.

Garnish with Vegan sour cream and serve warm.

Potatoes and Beans with Mustard

(Ready in about 40 minutes | Servings 4)

Ingredients

1 cup potatoes

1 ½ cups beans, canned in brine

2 teaspoon mustard

2 tablespoons olive oil

1/4 teaspoon turmeric powder

1 teaspoon cayenne pepper

1/2 teaspoon paprika

1/2 teaspoon Sea Salt

1/4 teaspoon black pepper

2 bay leaves

Directions

Prepare cooked potatoes. Cut potatoes in the cubes.

Place the potatoes in a large stockpot and cover them with two inches of water. Add the bay leaves.

Cook potatoes till they are tender. Drain the potatoes.

Heat the olive oil in a large iron-skillet, and add mustard. Cook mustard for 3 minutes.

Open the can and drain the beans.

Add potatoes and beans in a mustard sauce, season with salt, pepper and turmeric. Cook on high flame for a couple of minutes.

Add cayenne pepper, paprika and cook on low heat for 10 minutes. Serve warm.

Red Hot Chili Mushrooms

(Ready in about 30 minutes | Servings 2)

Ingredients

2 cups mushrooms, washed

2 tablespoons vegetable oil

1 large red onion, chopped

1 teaspoon fresh basil, chopped

1 sprig thyme

1/2 teaspoon salt

1/2 teaspoon Chili

2 large Tomatoes, sliced

1/3 cup tofu parmesan cheese, grated

Directions

Slice the mushrooms. Heat the oil in a large saucepan and sauté the onions. Add basil and thyme and cook till the onion is translucent and tender.

Add the sliced tomatoes and cook for 2 to 3 minutes, stirring constantly. Cut the mushrooms into slices and add them to the saucepan. Stir in thyme, salt and chili.

Reduce heat to law, cover and simmer for 15-20 minutes. Remove the lid and cook for few minutes to dry out the liquid.

Remove from the heat and place tofu parmesan on the top. Serve warm.

Chana (Chickpeas) in a Curry Sauce

(Ready in about 50 minutes | Servings 4)

Ingredients

1 cup potatoes

1 ½ cups chickpeas, canned in brine

4 tablespoon vegetable oil

2 cups curry sauce

2 teaspoon tomato sauce

1 teaspoon salt

1/4 teaspoon black pepper

1 teaspoon cayenne peeled

1 teaspoon coriander

1 teaspoon garam masala

1 teaspoon chilli powder

2 teaspoon green coriander, finely chopped

Directions

Boil potatoes with their skins. Cool them, peel, and cut into cubes.

Drain and rinse the chickpeas.

Heat the oil in a saucepan, add the curry sauce, and boil for about 4 minutes.

Stir in tomato sauce, salt, pepper, cayenne, coriander, garam masala and chili and mix well. Reduce the heat to low and simmer for 5 minutes, stirring constantly.

Add the boiled potatoes and green coriander. Mix all ingredients and serve warm.

PART THREE DINNER

Christmas Olivier Salad

(Ready in about 40 minutes | Servings 6)

Ingredients

5 medium potatoes

2 medium carrots, scraped

12 pickles

1/2 cup peas, canned and cooked

sea salt, to taste

ground pepper, to taste

1 tablespoons mustard

5 tablespoons vegan eggless mayonnaise

2 tablespoons non-dairy sour cream

olives for garnish (optional)

chopped parsley to taste, for garnish

Directions

In a large stockpot, cook the potatoes and carrots. When carrots are tender, remove them from the pot and continue to cook potatoes until they are tender.

Rinse the vegetables and dry them. Then, peel the boiled potatoes. Cut potatoes and carrots into small pieces and cool in a fridge.

Chop the pickled cucumbers as fine as possible.

Place potatoes, carrots, pickles and peas in a large mixing bowl. Season with salt and pepper (optional) and stir to mix well.

Stir in mustard, mayonnaise and sour cream, and mix well once again. Transfer to a serving bowl, sprinkle parsley and garnish with olives, if desired.

Refreshing Stir-Fry with Seitan

(Ready in about 30 minutes | Servings 4)

Ingredients

3 tablespoons olive oil

1 pound seitan, patted dry and cut into bite-size pieces

1/4 cup almonds, chopped

4 carrots, thinly sliced

1 tomato, thinly sliced

1/2 cup rice wine

1/2 cup water

1 tablespoon brown sugar

2 tablespoons lemon juice

2 tablespoons hoisin sauce

2 teaspoons cornstarch

1/4 teaspoon salt

1/4 teaspoon freshly ground black pepper

1/2 teaspoon red pepper flakes

Directions

Heat 2 tablespoons olive oil in a large heavy skillet or wok over medium flame. Add seitan, until it is crispy, for 5 minutes.

Add the remaining 1 tablespoon olive oil and chopped almonds. Cook, stirring constantly, about 1 minute. Add carrots and tomatoes, and cook, stirring often, about 1 to 2 minute.

To make a sauce: Mix rice wine, water, sugar, lemon juice, hoisin, cornstarch and salt in a deep mixing bowl. Whisk well to combine all ingredients.

Add the sauce to the pan and mix. Reduce flame to medium point, cover saucepan and cook until the vegetables are crisp and soft, 3 to 4 minutes.

Add black pepper and red pepper flakes and adjust the seasonings. When the sauce is thickened, the meal is ready to serve.

Divide your stir-fry among serving plates, sprinkle remaining almonds and serve hot.

Herby Tomato and Quinoa Salad

(Ready in about 30 minutes | Servings 4)

Ingredients

4 cups water

1 cup quinoa

1/2 cup onions, chopped

2 cloves garlic, minced

4 tomatoes, diced

2 tablespoons fresh parsley

1/2 cup toasted almonds

6 dried dates, chopped

3 tablespoons extra-virgin olive oil

2 tablespoons orange juice

2 teaspoons lemon zest

2 nutritional yeast flakes

1/4 teaspoon fine sea salt

1/2 teaspoon sage

1/4 teaspoon marjoram, dried

Directions

Bring the saucepan of the water to a boil. Add the quinoa and cook over medium flame for 10 minutes. Rinse, drain and reserve.

Combine onions, garlic, tomatoes, parsley, almonds and dates in a large salad bowl. Drizzle the oil and orange juice. Add lemon zest and yeast flakes. Sprinkle salt, sage and marjoram.

Stir in the quinoa and place to the fridge. Stir before serving and serve chilled.

Fluffy-Chewy Peanut Pizza

(Ready in about 40 minutes + 3 hours for dough | Servings 6)

Ingredients

Pizza Dough

3 cups white wheat flour

1 teaspoon salt

2 teaspoons honey

2 teaspoons instant yeast

11/4 cups warm water (110 to 120°F)

2 tablespoons vegetable oil

Pizza Ingredients

2/3 cup peanut butter

1/3 cup hoisin sauce

1 tablespoon hot sauce

3/4 to 1 cup shredded vegan mozzarella

1/2 cup broccoli florets, chopped

1/2 cup mushrooms

1 small bunch spring leeks, thinly sliced

1 teaspoon oregano

fresh basil leaves

Directions

To prepare the dough: Sift the flour, and add salt and honey in a large mixing bowl. Put the yeast (at a room temperature) into dry mixture, then add the water and oil, and stir with the fork until all ingredients are combined well.

If the dough seems dry, add a little more water. Cover the bowl with fitted lid, and let sit in a warm place to rise for about 3 hours.

Preheat the oven to 500 degrees F.

Mix the peanut butter, hoisin sauce, 1/4 cup hot water and hot sauce. Whisk until the sauce is creamy. Reserve.

Stretch and roll out the dough on floured surface. Spread the sauce evenly on the pizza, layer the cheese and then top with the broccoli and mushrooms. Sprinkle leeks and oregano.

Place the pizza on a baking sheet with parchment paper. Bake for 15 minutes until the cheese is melted.

Let sit to cool for 5 minutes, arrange with basil leaves and serve hot.

Flatbread Sandwiches with Chickpea Salad

(Ready in about 30 minutes | Servings 4)

Ingredients

2 cups cooked chickpeas

1 small onion, chopped

1 large stalk celery, chopped

2 tablespoons tofu cream cheese

2 tablespoons lemon juice

1 large carrot, shredded

1/2 teaspoon salt

1/4 teaspoon black pepper

1/2 teaspoon dried dill

Wholemeal flatbreads

lettuce leaves

1 cucumber, sliced

Directions

Put onions, celery, tofu and lemon juice in an electric blender and mix until the mixture is chopped well. Add chickpeas, salt, pepper and dill, and blend a bit more.

Transfer the mixture in a bowl and add shredded carrot. Stir to combine.

Put prepared chickpea salad on the wholemeal flatbreads, arrange with lettuce leaves and cucumber slices, and serve.

Rich Multivitamin Stir-Fry

(Ready in about 25 minutes | Servings 4)

Ingredients

2 tablespoons olive oil

1 julienned green bell pepper, seeded and sliced

1 julienned yellow bell pepper, seeded and sliced

1 medium onion, chopped

1 clove garlic, minced

1 cup yellow squash, sliced

1 small eggplant, sliced

1 cup firm tofu, cut into large chunks

2 tablespoons soy sauce

2 tablespoons rice vinegar

1 teaspoon sugar

2 cups bok choy, sliced

1 cup bean sprouts

1/2 cup chickpeas, cooked

1/4 teaspoon sea salt

1/4 teaspoon smoked paprika

1/4 teaspoon freshly ground black pepper

2 tablespoons sesame oil

1 bunch parsley

Directions

In a wide and deep heavy skillet, heat the olive oil over high-medium flame.

Sauté the peppers, onion and garlic, stirring frequently. Add squash, eggplant, tofu, soy sauce, vinegar and sugar, stirring often for. Cook until the vegetables are half-cooked.

Add the bok choy and sprouts, season with salt, pepper and smoked paprika, and cook, stirring frequently for about 2 minutes longer. Add sesame oil.

Stir in chickpeas and cook for about 30 seconds. Arrange with parsley and serve warm.

Vegan Caesar Salad

(Ready in about 20 minutes | Servings 1)

Ingredients

2 cloves garlic, crushed

1/2 teaspoon salt

1 tablespoon Dijon mustard

2 tablespoons lemon juice

1 teaspoon vegetarian Vegan Worcestershire sauce

1 tablespoon dry white wine

1/4 teaspoon fresh ground black pepper

1/2 cup olive oil

1 head butter lettuce

1/4 cup vegan Parmesan

1/4 cup croutons

Directions

Combine the garlic and salt, mix well and allow them to sit together for 2 minutes. Then add the mustard, lemon juice, Worcestershire and wine. Add freshly ground black pepper.

Drizzle in the oil very carefully, and then drizzle a little faster because the oil should be well incorporated.

Remove and discard the tough outer lettuce leaves. Wash the lettuce thoroughly.

Use large salad bowl. Combine lettuce, vegan Parmesan and croutons. Add the dressing and serve immediately.

Mesclun Greens with Raisins, Cashews and Almonds

(Ready in about 25 minutes | Servings 4)

Ingredients

1/8 cup sliced cashew nuts

1/8 cup almond

ginger two slices

4 cups mesclun greens

1/2 cup raisins

Directions

Preheat the oven to 300 degrees F. Toast the cashew nuts and almonds for 8 minutes, or till they are golden.

Remove from the oven and set aside. Cut the ginger into very thin strips.

Put the mesclun greens in a large salad bowl and drizzle the dressing equally.

Sprinkle the cashew, almonds and ginger on top of prepared salad. Garnish with raisins.

Christmas Dinner Potato Salad

(Ready in about 30 minutes + cooling for 40 minutes | Servings 6)

Ingredients

2 pounds fingerling potatoes, scrubbed and cut into cubes

2 large carrots, cut into matchsticks

1 tablespoon capers

1 tablespoon Dijon mustard

1/2 cup red wine vinegar

2 teaspoons lemon juice

1 large red onion, sliced

1 large green onion, sliced

1 clove garlic, minced

1 teaspoons minced fresh tarragon

1 teaspoon basil

1/2 cup olive oil

1/2 teaspoon kosher salt

1/4 teaspoon freshly ground pepper

1 tablespoon minced fresh parsley

10 black olives

Directions

Cook the potatoes and carrots in a large stockpot of water till they are fork tender. Drain and rinse the vegetables and rinse through cold water to avoid discoloration. Let the vegetables cool.

Take a half of the capers and put in a large mixing bowl. Add the mustard, wine vinegar, lemon juice, onions, garlic, tarragon and basil, and mix all ingredients well.

Then prepare the dressing. Drizzle the oil into the mixture, slowly at first, and then. The dressing must be fairly thick, almost as much as mayonnaise.

Add the potatoes and the remaining capers and toss until all of the vegetables are coated.

Season with salt and freshly ground pepper. Refrigerate to allow the flavors to blend before serving. Before serving time, sprinkle fresh parsley and arrange with olives.

Herb bread with Vegetables

(Ready in about 20 minutes | Servings 6)

Ingredients

6 slices fresh herb bread

2 carrots, scraped and grated

4 spring onions, finely sliced

2 cups sugar snap peas

1/2 cup tomatoes, halved

2 tablespoons fresh Thai basil leaves

2 red chili peppers, finely chopped

1/2 cup non-diary milk

2 tablespoons apple vinegar

2 teaspoons olive oil

sea salt to taste

freshly ground black pepper to taste

1 sprig Rosemary for garnish

Directions

Combine the carrots, onions, peas and tomatoes in a mixing bowl. Tear basil leaves into pieces and add to the vegetables in the mixing bowl.

Put chili peppers, milk, vinegar, olive oil, salt and pepper in a jar, cover and shake vigorously until all ingredients are well blended.

Pour the dressing over the vegetables, mix well, and adjust the seasonings.

Spread the vegetables on slices of bread, sprinkle chopped rosemary and serve immediately.

Snow Peas Stir-Fry with Szechuan Tofu

(Ready in about 30 minutes | Servings 4)

Ingredients

1/4 cup soy sauce

1 tablespoon tomato sauce

1 teaspoon balsamic vinegar

1 tablespoon maple syrup

1/2 teaspoon cayenne pepper

3 tablespoons cornstarch

1 (14-ounce) package Szechuan tofu, drained

2 tablespoons grape seed oil

4 cups snow peas

4 cloves garlic, minced

1 teaspoon dry ginger powder

1/2 teaspoon kosher salt

1/4 teaspoon red pepper flakes

Directions

Combine soy sauce, tomato sauce, balsamic vinegar, maple syrup, 1/4 cup water, cayenne and 1 teaspoon cornstarch in a medium mixing bowl. Reserve.

Chop tofu into bite-sized cubes and pat dry. Stir in tofu in a mixing bowl and add remaining 2 tablespoons cornstarch.

Heat 1 tablespoon oil in a wide and deep iron-skillet over medium heat. Add the tofu pieces and cook for 2 minutes. Flip and stir carefully. Cook until the tofu is golden browned and crispy, or 3 minutes more. Remove to a serving plate.

Add the remaining 1 tablespoon oil to the pan. Add snow peas, garlic and ginger, and season with salt and pepper. Cook, stirring frequently, for 1 to 2 minutes.

Add 1/4 cup water more, cover and cook until the peas are tender or 3 minutes. Stir in the prepared sauce. Cook until they are thickened.

Add the tofu and cook, stirring occasionally, until heated through. Serve immediately.

Couscous with Griddled Onion Rings

(Ready in about 1 hour | Servings 4)

Ingredients

1 lb. couscous	1/4 teaspoon salt
4 onions	1/8 black pepper
Vegetable oil, for griddling	1/4 teaspoon smoked paprika
2 tablespoons balsamic vinegar	1/4 cup Vegan Barbecue Sauce

Directions

Place the couscous in a deep bowl, and add warm water to cover the surface of grains. Put the lid and let stand for 30 minutes in a warm place.

Cut the onions into rings.

Brush a griddle with oil, and heat the griddle until it is hot. Grill the onion rings slices for 4 minutes on each side.

Plump up the grains of couscous with a fork. Drizzle balsamic vinegar and add salt, pepper and paprika. Taste and adjust seasonings.

Transfer the couscous in four warm plates. Top the couscous with warm onion rings, and pour vegan barbecue sauce over your meal. Serve immediately.

Roasted Mini Club Sandwiches

(Ready in about 30 minutes | Servings 4)

Ingredients

2 cloves garlic, minced

1 ½ cups cooked cannellini beans, rinsed and drained

3/4 cup water

1 teaspoon lime juice

1 teaspoon ground coriander

1 teaspoon sea salt

Freshly ground black pepper (optional)

1 medium red bell peppers, seeded and sliced

1 medium tomato, sliced

3 small onions, cut into rings

2 tablespoons canola oil

2 teaspoon eggless mayonnaise

Square Bread slices

Directions

To prepare bean spread, heat oil in a wide skillet over high-medium heat. Add garlic and cook 2 minutes.

Add beans and stir in 3/4 cup water, add coriander and cook for 10 minutes, stirring often. Stir in lime juice. Reserve.

Make sandwiches on the following way: Place bean spread on each bread slice. Add mayonnaise and scatter bell peppers, tomatoes and onions equally. Sprinkle salt and pepper.

Preheat the oven to 300 degrees F. Bake prepared sandwiches until the vegetables are crispy and tender. Cut baked sandwiches in half diagonally and serve immediately.

Eggplant Pizza with Tomato-Garlic Sauce

(Ready in about 40 minutes | Servings 4)

Ingredients

1 (28-ounce) can diced plum tomatoes

2 tablespoons extra-virgin olive oil

4 large cloves garlic, minced

1 teaspoon dried oregano

1 teaspoon dried basil

1/2 large eggplant, cut thin slices

2 tablespoons oil

1 (14 ounce) package prebaked pizza crust

3/4 cup shredded non-diary mozzarella cheese

Directions

Prepare Tomato-Garlic sauce on the following way. Mix the tomatoes, oil, garlic, oregano and basil. Blend all ingredients until the sauce is smooth. Reserve.

Coat the slices of eggplant with salt and put in a colander. Set aside for at least 30 minutes. After that, thoroughly rinse the eggplant slices and pat it dry.

Preheat a heavy skillet, add 2 tablespoons oil and cook slices of eggplant, for 4 minutes on each side.

Preheat the oven (preferably with a pizza stone) to 500 degrees F.

Line a large baking sheet with parchment paper or aluminum foil. Place pizza crust on the baking sheet.

Spread the sauce evenly on the pizza. Then, sprinkle the mozzarella and cover with eggplant slices.

Transfer the pizza on the baking sheet, and bake for 10 to 15 minutes, till the cheese is melted and the crust is dark brown.

Basmati and Veggies Stir-Fry

(Ready in about 40 minutes | Servings 2)

Ingredients

1 cup instant basmati rice

1 cup vegetable stock

3 teaspoons canola oil

2/3 cup asparagus spears, cut into bite-sized pieces

1 medium green bell pepper, thinly sliced

1 medium leek, sliced

1 clove garlic, minced

1 tablespoon fresh ginger, minced

4 teaspoons tamari soy sauce

1 tablespoon rice vinegar

1 tablespoon lime juice

1/2 teaspoon kosher salt

1/4 teaspoon black pepper

1/4 teaspoon red pepper flakes

1 tablespoon toasted sesame seeds

Directions

Place rice and vegetable stock in a wide and deep skillet. Bring prepared stock to a boil over high flame. Reduce flame to medium and simmer until the liquid is evaporated, or about 13 minutes. Remove from skillet and reserve.

While the cooked rice is cooling, heat 1 tablespoon oil in the skillet over high-medium heat. Cook for 1 minute, stirring often. Set aside.

Heat remaining 2 tablespoons oil in the skillet over medium flame. Add asparagus and cook, for 2 minutes. Add bell pepper, leeks, garlic, and ginger. Cook 2 to 3 minutes, or until the vegetables are crisp and tender.

Place the cooked rice, tamari sauce, vinegar, lime juice in the skillet. Season with salt and pepper and cook for 2 minutes. Taste and adjust the seasonings.

Transfer to a serving platter, sprinkle red pepper flakes and sesame seeds and serve immediately.

Cabbage-Corn Salad with Pineapple

(Ready in about 20 minutes | Servings 4)

Ingredients

2 tablespoons extra-virgin olive oil

1 teaspoon apple cider vinegar

1 teaspoon maple syrup

1/2 teaspoon sea salt

black pepper, to taste

1 cup cabbage, shredded

1/2 cup corn kernels

1 cup pineapple, diced

1/2 cup tomato, cut into bite-sized pieces

2 cups romaine leaves

1/4 cup onion, cut into rings

1 teaspoon lemon zest

1/4 teaspoon cumin seeds

Directions

To prepare salad dressing, whisk olive oil, vinegar, maple syrup, salt and pepper in a jar. Mix vigorously to combine all ingredients.

Place cabbage, corn, pineapple, tomato, romaine, onion and lemon zest in a mixing bowl and stir to combine. Pour the dressing over vegetables. Taste salad and adjust seasonings.

Divide salad among serving bowls, sprinkle cumin seeds and decorate with lemon slices.

Coconut meat with Salad and Tahini Dressing

(Ready in about 20 minutes | Servings 4)

Ingredients

2 cups Thai baby coconut meat

2 tablespoons Bragg Liquid Aminos

2 tablespoons olive oil

1/2 cup sesame seeds

1/2 teaspoon minced garlic

1/2 teaspoon sea salt

1/2 cup tahini

1 tablespoon Nama Shoyu

1 1/2 tablespoons apple cider vinegar

2 teaspoons maple syrup

1/3 cup water, as needed

2 tablespoons fresh basil, chopped

2 cups daikon radish, shredded

1/4 cup cucumbers, sliced

1/4 cup red bell pepper, sliced

Directions

To prepare coconut meat, mix coconut with Bragg Liquid Aminos and olive oil.

Crush sesame seeds by using a mortar and pestle. Divide sesame onto bowl and dip each piece of coconut meat into sesame.

Transfer the pieces on dehydrator trays. Dry at 104 degrees F for at least 6 hours.

To prepare dressing, mash garlic and salt by using a mortar and pestle. Add tahini, Nama Shoyu, vinegar, maple syrup and mix all ingredients well. Add water gradually to desired consistency. Sprinkle the basil.

Place radish, cucumber and bell pepper in a large bowl. Add dressing and stir to mix well.

Divide salad among serving plates and arrange with coconut meat and serve.

Pita bread with Garlic Cream

(Ready in about 20 minutes | Servings 4)

Ingredients

4 slices bread, crusts removed

1 tablespoon tahini

2 garlic cloves, minced

2 tablespoons lemon juice

1/2 cup olive oil

1/4 teaspoon salt

1/8 teaspoon black pepper

4 pitas, split in half

Romaine leaves

Toasted almonds for garnish.

Directions

Tear the bread slices into chunks. Put the bread, tahini, garlic cloves and lemon juice in a food processor, and blend to a coarse paste. While you blend ingredients, slowly add the olive oil dropwise.

Place prepared cream to a bowl, season with salt and pepper, and add sesame seeds.

Cut each pita in halves horizontally. Place a romaine leaf inside each half, spread a little garlic cream and arrange with almonds.

Roasted Sweet Potatoes with Tahini Sauce

(Ready in about 1 hour | Servings 4)

Ingredients

3 medium sweet potatoes

1 (15-ounce) can chickpeas, rinsed and drained

1 tablespoon vegetable oil

1/2 teaspoon cumin,

1/2 teaspoon paprika

1/4 teaspoon salt

1 teaspoon lemon zest

1/4 cup tahini

3 cloves garlic, minced

A small amount of water

1/4 cup fresh parsley, chopped

Directions

Line a baking sheet with parchment paper or Silpat baking mat. Preheat oven to 400 degrees F.

Wash and scrub potatoes. Then cut them in halves lengthwise.

Rinse and drain chickpeas. Drizzle olive oil and add spices and place on the baking sheet. Place sweet potatoes face down on the baking sheet and roast vegetables for 30 minutes, or until potatoes are fork tender and golden on top.

Meanwhile, prepare the sauce by adding oil, spices, lemon zest, tahini, garlic and water to a large bowl. Whisk all ingredients, taste and adjust the seasonings.

Remove potatoes and chickpeas from the oven. Top potatoes with chickpeas and tahini sauce. Sprinkle parsley and serve warm.

Iceberg-Sprouts Salad with Mayonnaise

(Ready in about 20 minutes | Servings 2)

Ingredients

1 medium apple, peeled, and diced	3 cups iceberg lettuce leaves
1/3 cup apple cider vinegar	1/2 carrots, grated
1/2 cup olive oil	1 small julienned cucumbers
1 tablespoon agave syrup	1/2 cup radish sprouts
1/3 cup parsley	2 tablespoons alfalfa sprouts
1/8 teaspoon sea salt	1/2 cup chickpeas
1/8 teaspoon black pepper	2 tablespoons vegan eggless mayonnaise
1/4 teaspoon basil	Olives (optional)

Directions

Mix apple, vinegar, olive oil, agave syrup, parsley, salt, pepper and basil in a bowl of an electric blender. Mix until dressing is smooth.

Place iceberg lettuce, carrot, cucumber, radish sprouts, alfalfa sprouts and chickpeas in a large bowl. Pour the prepared dressing over vegetables and mix gently.

Divide prepared salad among serving plates and garnish with mayonnaise and olives.

Fried Veggies with smoked Tofu

(Ready in about 30 minutes | Servings 6)

Ingredients

1/2 cup vegetable stock

1/4 cup rice wine

3 tablespoons soy sauce

3 tablespoons cornstarch

2 tablespoons maple syrup

11/2 cup smoked tofu, cut into bite-sized chunks

1/4 teaspoon salt

1/4 teaspoon freshly ground black pepper

1/4 teaspoon smoked paprika

2 tablespoons grape seed oil

2 cloves garlic, minced

6 cups cauliflower florets

2 cups White Button mushrooms, sliced

Directions

To make a sauce, whisk vegetable stock, wine, soy sauce, 1 tablespoon cornstarch and maple syrup in a mixing bowl, until all ingredients are combined. Reserve.

Cut smoked tofu into chunks and pat dry, season it with salt. Add the remaining 2 tablespoons cornstarch in another mixing bowl. Add the tofu and mix carefully.

Heat 1 tablespoon oil in a wide nonstick skillet over medium-high flame. Add the tofu, and cook, until the tofu is browned, about 3 to 4 minutes. Gently flip and continue to cook the other side for 3 minutes more.

Reduce heat to medium. Add the remaining 1 tablespoon oil and garlic. Cook until it is fragrant. Add cauliflower florets, mushrooms and a few tablespoons of water.

Season with salt and pepper, cover and cook, stirring occasionally, for 3 minutes longer. Stir in the sauce. Cook until the sauce is thickened, for about 2 minutes.

Remove from heat and combine with tofu, vegetables, and sauce. Sprinkle smoked paprika, adjust seasonings and serve warm.

Veggie Cutlet with Smoked Tofu

(Ready in about 1 hour | Servings 4)

Ingredients

2 medium potatoes, peeled

1 medium leek, sliced

1 large carrot, grated

1/2 cup beans

1/2 teaspoon sea salt

1/4 teaspoon freshly ground black pepper

1 teaspoon coriander, chopped

1 teaspoon Chili powder

1/2 teaspoon garlic powder

1/4 cup corn flour

1/4 cup bread crumbs

Vegetable Oil for frying

1 cup smoked tofu, cut into bite-sized cubes

A bunch fresh parsley

Directions

Bring a stockpot of water to boil, and boil potato. Then mash potatoes well. Set aside.

Heat the oil in a saucepan and sauté the leeks until it is translucent. Add grated carrot, and beans. Continue cooking for 5 minutes.

Season with salt and pepper, add coriander, chili and garlic powder.

Add the cooked vegetable mixture to mashed potatoes and mix to combine all ingredients.

Form prepared mixture into small patties.

Mix a small amount of water with corn flour and make a thick paste. Dip the vegetable patties in the paste. Then, dip the patties into bread crumbs.

Heat the oil in a saucepan over medium-high flame, and shallow fry the patties. Put fried cutlets on a paper napkin to soak up excess oil. Transfer on a serving platter and garnish with smoked tofu cubes. Tear the parsley leaves and sprinkle parsley over cutlets.

Broccoli-Peanut Patties with Sour Cream

(Ready in about 45 minutes | Servings 4)

Ingredients

1 small head broccoli

1/2 cup alfalfa sprouts

2 green onions, finely sliced

2 cloves garlic, minced

1/2 cup vegan peanut butter

2 teaspoons fresh basil leaves, chopped

1 teaspoon cumin

2 teaspoon extra-virgin olive oil

1/2 cup wheat germ

1/2 cup non-dairy sour cream

Directions

Chop broccoli into florets and stalks. Blend the broccoli, alfalfa sprouts, onions, and garlic in a food processor or an electric blender, till they are finely chopped and almost creamy.

Mix together prepared vegetable mixture with the vegan peanut butter, basil and cumin, till they are not too sticky and not too humid. Using your hands, form the mixture into 4 patties.

Heat the oil in a wide and deep saucepan over medium-high flame.

Dredge the patties in the wheat germ. Fry the patties shortly until they are crisp on each surface. Make sure that they will not become gooey.

Divide patties among serving plates, arrange with sour cream and serve warm.

Dinner Party Barbecue

(Ready in about 35 minutes | Servings 4)

Ingredients

1 medium red onion, peeled

2 leeks

2 cloves garlic, peeled

1 large red bell pepper, seeded

1 large green bell pepper, seeded

1 zucchini, trimmed

2 teaspoons oil

1 ½ cup barbecue sauce

4 sandwich rolls

Directions

Cut the onions and leeks into halves lengthwise. Finely chop the garlic. Cut the peppers into thin strips. Cut the zucchini into ribbons.

Heat the oil over medium-high flame in a grill pan. When the oil begins to smoke, sauté the onion and garlic, until the onion is soft. Then, add the peppers.

Add the zucchini ribbons to the grill pan and cook until they are tender.

Then, pour the barbecue sauce over the vegetables. Divide the barbecue between sandwich rolls, garnish with favorite salads and serve warm.

Pizza with Noodles and Cashew Cheese

(Ready in about 1 hour | Servings 4)

Ingredients

1/2 cup raw cashews

1/4 cup nutritional yeast flakes

1 teaspoon granulated onion

1 teaspoon paprika

1 teaspoon salt

2 cups of water

1 package prebaked pizza crust

1 ¼ cup cooked macaroni noodles

1 (15-ounce) can vegan chili

1 cup shredded vegan mozzarella-style cheese

Chopped corn chips, for garnish

Chopped fresh rosemary, for garnish

Directions

Prepare Cashew cheese sauce. In the bowl of a blender, combine 2 cups of water, the cashews, nutritional yeast, onion, paprika, and salt. Process the mixture at high speed until it is smooth. Pour the prepared mixture into a deep saucepan and bring to a simmer over law-medium heat, stirring continuously. Cooking will take about15 minutes.

Preheat the oven to 500 degrees F.

In a mixing bowl, combine together the cooked pasta and the cashew sauce. Set aside.

In a small skillet bring the vegan chili to a simmer.

Place the pizza crust to a large sheet of parchment paper. Spread the mozzarella evenly over the crust, then spread the macaroni noodles over it. Top with prepared chili.

Transfer the pizza with parchment paper on the baking sheets. Bake for 15 minutes. Check the pizza to see if the cheese is melted and the crust is slightly brown. Bake for a few more minutes if necessary.

Decorate the pizza with corn chips and chopped fresh rosemary, cut into pieces and serve hot.

Multicolored Summer Salad with Tahini

(Ready in about 1 hour | Servings 2)

Ingredients

3/4 cup tahini

1/2 cup lemon juice

1/3 cup Bragg Liquid Aminos

1/2 cup water

1 cup cherry tomatoes

1/2 cup radish

1/2 cup bean sprouts

1 sliced cucumber

4 cups butter lettuce

1/3 cup fresh mint, whole leaves

1 cup rye croutons

Directions

Put tahini, lemon juice, Bragg Liquid Aminos and water in a blender bowl. Process to mix well and shake all flavors.

Place tomatoes, radish, bean sprouts and cucumber in a large mixing bowl. Pour the dressing over salad. Add lettuce leaves.

Arrange with fresh mint leaves and croutons.

You can keep this salad covered, for 3 days in a fridge.

Thai Papaya Salad

(Ready in about 20 minutes | Servings 4)

Ingredients

1 teaspoon garlic

1/2 teaspoon red chili pepper, chopped

1/2 cup chopped green bean,

1 tablespoon Bragg Liquid Aminos

1 teaspoon salt

3 tablespoons lemon juice

2 tablespoons maple syrup

2 tablespoons chopped almonds

2 cups green papaya, peeled and shredded

1 carrot, shredded

1/2 cup fresh cabbage, shredded

1/2 cup cherry tomatoes

2 tablespoons roasted almonds

2 tablespoons dried cranberries

Directions

To prepare dressing, blend garlic and chili in an electric processor. Add green beans, Bragg Liquid Aminos, lemon, maple syrup and almonds, and mix well to combine all ingredients.

Place papaya, carrots, cabbage and tomatoes in a large mixing bowl. Season with salt and toss with prepared dressing.

Sprinkle with almond and cranberries and serve right away.

You can help papaya salads stay fresh for 2 days by storing them in your fridge, when it is stored without dressing.

Spicy Vegetable Cutlets

(Ready in about 35 minutes | Servings 4)

Ingredients

3 large potatoes, peeled

1/2 cup green peas

1/3 cup sweet corn

1/2 cup carrot, grated

1/4 cup beans

1/3 cup beetroot, grated

2 green onions, thinly sliced

1/2 teaspoon salt

1/4 teaspoon black pepper

1/2 teaspoon paprika

1/4 teaspoon red pepper flakes

1/4 teaspoon garlic powder

1/4 teaspoon turmeric powder

1/2 teaspoon Garam Masala powder

1 teaspoon balsamic vinegar

1/2 cup bread crumbs

2 tablespoons corn flour

vegetable oil for shallow frying

Directions

Boil peeled potatoes in a deep stockpot until they are fork tender.

Put green peas, sweet corn, carrot and beans in a deep and wide saucepan or wok, cover and cook them for 10 minutes over medium flame. Drain vegetables to remove excess water.

Heat the nonstick pan over high-medium flame. Add chopped green onions and stir-fry until it is translucent.

Add prepared vegetables and beetroot, and season with salt, pepper, pepper flakes and paprika. Cook for 3 to 4 minutes, stirring often. Add garlic powder, turmeric powder, garam masala powder and stir to mix well.

Transfer prepared mixture in a large mixing bowl. Add boiled potatoes, 1/4 cup bread crumbs and vinegar. Mix well and adjust seasonings if required.

Divide prepared mixture into equal patties of the desired size. To make patties, you can take one portion, make a round shape of ball and flatten it.

Place remaining 1/4 cup bread crumbs in a plate. Make a paste by mixing corn flour and 4 tablespoons water in a mixing bowl. Dip patties in flour batter and roll and coat with breadcrumbs.

Heat the oil in a saucepan or griddle over medium heat. Place patties and cook until they are golden brown. Turn and cook another side for 4 minutes more. Transfer cutlets over kitchen absorbent paper to absorb excess oil. Serve immediately.

Tzatziki Breaded Eggplant with Tomato sauce

(Ready in about 1 hour | Servings 4)

Ingredients

1 medium eggplant, cut into slices	2 tablespoons vegetable oil
Salt	1/4 teaspoon black pepper
1/2 cup non-dairy milk	1 teaspoon dried oregano
1/4 cup cornstarch	1 teaspoon spice mix for Tzatziki
11/2 cups panko breadcrumbs	Tomato sauce to taste
2 tablespoons nutritional yeast flakes	

Directions

Remove the peel from eggplant and cut eggplant into thin slices. Sprinkle with salt and put in a colander. Set aside for about 30 minutes. After that, thoroughly rinse the eggplant slices and pat dry.

Combine vegan milk and cornstarch and stir to mix. Coat the eggplant slices with the milk mixture, then coat with the panko crumbs evenly and add yeast flakes.

Prepare a large baking sheet, line it with parchment paper. Layer the slices on the baking sheet, drizzle the oil, season with pepper, oregano and spice mix for Tzatziki, and bake.

Once the eggplant is browned and crisp, flip the slices over, and bake until the second side is browned.

Remove baked eggplant slices on a serving plates and garnish with tomato sauce.

Onion-Orange Salad with Mint

(Ready in about 30 minutes | Servings 2)

Ingredients

2 tablespoons lemon juice

1 tablespoon balsamic vinegar

1/4 teaspoon salt

1/2 teaspoon sugar

1 tablespoon fresh mint leaves, chopped

3 tablespoons extra-virgin olive oil

1 large onion

3 large oranges

10 black olives

Directions

Prepare the dressing. Whisk the lemon juice, vinegar, salt, and sugar. Add the olive oil and mix well. Add the chopped mint leaves. Set aside.

Cut the onion into thin slices. Soak the onion slices in cold water for 10-15 minutes. Toss with 2 tablespoons of prepared dressing. Reserve.

Meanwhile, peel the oranges and cut them crosswise into 1/4-inch-thick slices. Sprinkle the orange slices with the remaining dressing.

Arrange the orange and onion slices in a serving platter and garnish with black olives.

Basil, Hazelnuts and Mushroom Pizza

(Ready in about 1 hour + 3 hours for dough | Servings 6)

Ingredients

1/2 cup fresh basil leaves

1/3 cup roasted hazelnuts

4 cloves garlic

2 tablespoons nutritional yeast flakes

1/2 teaspoon kosher salt

Black pepper to taste

1/4 cup olive oil

2 cups white wheat flour

1 cup all-purpose flour

1 teaspoon salt

2 tablespoons sugar

2 teaspoons instant yeast, at room temperature

2 tablespoons olive oil

1/2 cup Tomato Sauce

2 tablespoons spicy ketchup

1 cup cremini mushrooms, sliced

1 teaspoon oregano

Directions

Combine together the basil, hazelnuts, garlic, yeast, salt and pepper. Blend in a food processor and then add the olive oil slowly, until the basil sauce is smooth and creamy. Adjust the seasonings.

Prepare the pizza dough. Mix the flours, salt, and sugar in a large mixing bowl. Put the yeast on top of the dry mixture, then add the 1 ¼ cups warm water (120°F) and oil. Stir until all ingredients are combined well.

If the dough is dry, add a little more water. Cover the bowl with fitted lid, and allow to rise at a warm place for at least 3 hours.

Preheat the oven to 500 degrees F. Overlay the baking sheets with a parchment paper.

Stretch and roll out pizza dough on a floured surface. Feel free to dust with additional flour if the dough seems sticky. Transfer the dough on the baking sheets. Spread the tomato sauce and ketchup over the dough and top with mushrooms. Sprinkle oregano and adjust the seasonings.

Bake for 15 minutes, or till the pizza dough is darkish brown. Let your pizza cool for a few minutes, and then cut into squares and serve warm.

Sesame Carrot and Cucumber Salad

(Ready in about 30 minutes | Servings 2)

Ingredients

2 teaspoons extra-virgin olive oil

2 teaspoons ginger, grated

2 cloves garlic, minced

2 teaspoons tamarind paste

2 tablespoons apple cider vinegar

2 tablespoons water

2 large carrots, shredded

1 cucumber, finely sliced

1 teaspoons sesame seeds

1 teaspoon flax seeds

1/2 teaspoon salt

1/4 teaspoon black pepper

1/4 teaspoon rosemary

Directions

Heat the oil in a wok over high-medium flame, then add the ginger and garlic, and cook until they are fragrant.

To prepare sauce: Add the tamarind paste, vinegar and water, stirring frequently and cook for 10 minutes. Add the carrots and cook for a few minutes.

Place the cucumber in a large mixing bowl, add the carrots and prepared sauce, and toss all together. Season with salt and pepper

Sprinkle the sesame seeds and flax seeds.

Chill for at least 1 hour, sprinkle rosemary and stir before serving.

Chopped Vegetable Salad

(Ready in about 30 minutes | Servings 4)

Ingredients

1 cup cauliflower florets, blanched and chopped

2 tomatoes, diced

1 medium cucumber, sliced

1 small yellow bell pepper, seeded and slice

1 small red bell pepper, seeded and sliced

1 small red onion, sliced

2 cups romaine lettuce, cut into 1 ½ -inch squares

1/2 teaspoon sea salt

1/4 freshly ground pepper

1/3 cup extra virgin olive oil

2 tablespoons lemon juice

1 tablespoon apple vinegar

1 teaspoon cumin

Lemon slices if desired

Toasted bread, if desired

Directions

Combine all vegetables in a mixing bowl. Season with sea salt and pepper. Mix well till the salt is good dissolved.

Drizzle the oil on the salad and toss to combine.

Add the lemon juice and vinegar, and mix again. Divide in a few serving plates and sprinkle cumin. Arrange with lemon slices. Serve with toasted bread if desired.

Asian Coleslaw with Almonds

(Ready in about 40 minutes | Servings 6)

Ingredients

3 tablespoons lime juice

2 tablespoons balsamic vinegar

1/2 teaspoon salt

1 tablespoon sugar

2 dried red chilies

4 cups cabbage, sliced

1 small carrot, grated

2 spring leeks, sliced

1 small beet, grated

1 tablespoon fresh ginger, minced

1/4 cup almonds, toasted

cilantro leaves for garnish

1 teaspoon cumin (optional)

Directions

Combine the lime juice, vinegar, salt, and sugar in a mixing bowl. Add chilies, cabbage, carrots, leeks, beet and ginger. Mix all ingredients thoroughly.

Let it stand for 15 minutes to allow the flavors and juices to mix slowly.

Divide the salad among serving plates. Chop the almonds. Sprinkle your salad with almonds and cumin.

Garnish with whole cilantro leaves and serve immediately.

Creamy Tofu Potato Salad

(Ready in about 30 minutes + cooling for 3 hours | Servings 6)

Ingredients

2 pounds lady christl potatoes, scrubbed and cut into cubes

2 stalks celery, sliced

1 cup vegan mayonnaise

1 tablespoon mustard

1 tablespoon vinegar

2 teaspoons lemon juice

1 teaspoon lemon zest

1/4 teaspoon salt

1/4 teaspoon freshly ground black pepper

1 large onion, finely sliced

1/2 cup shallots, sliced into rings

1 tablespoon olive oil

1/2 cup firm tofu, cubed

Directions

Place potatoes and celery in a stockpot and cover them with cold water. Bring the stockpot to boil and then reduce heat to low. Cover and cook for 25 minutes, till potatoes and celery are fork tender. Drain and cool them.

Meanwhile, prepare creamy sauce. Combine mayonnaise, mustard, vinegar, lemon juice, lemon zest, salt and pepper.

Place prepared potatoes and celery in a large mixing bowl (preferably glass bowl), and add onions and shallots. Drizzle the olive oil on them and toss to combine.

Pour prepared creamy sauce and toss again. Cover the salad bowl and refrigerate at least 3 hours. Scatter tofu cubes over the top and serve cool.

Summer Night Vegan Barbecue

(Ready in about 1 hour | Servings 3)

Ingredients

3 green onions,

1 large red bell pepper, seeded

1 large yellow bell pepper, seeded

1 large green bell pepper, seeded

3 corncobs

10 portobello mushrooms

2 teaspoons oil

1/2 teaspoon salt

1/4 teaspoon freshly ground black pepper

1 tablespoon fresh parsley, chopped

1 small can tomato sauce

2 tablespoons maple syrup

1 tablespoon apple vinegar

2 tablespoons soy sauce or

1 teaspoon paprika

1 teaspoon dried basil

Directions

Prepare 1 1/2 cups of homemade BBQ sauce on the following way:

Combine tomato sauce, maple syrup, vinegar, soy sauce, paprika, and basil, and stir well to mix flavors. Cover and let stand for an hour for better results.

Wash the vegetables and prepare for your barbecue. Cut the peppers and mushrooms into halves vertically. Drizzle the olive oil.

Preheat the grill and place the vegetables. Corncobs will need to bake longer than the other vegetables. Grill the vegetables until they are tender-crisp.

Remove the vegetables from grill to a serving platter. Season with salt and pepper, and pour barbecue sauce over vegetables. Sprinkle chopped parsley and serve hot.

Pasta Salad with Peppers in Vinaigrette

(Ready in about 30 minutes + 1 hour for cooling | Servings 4)

Ingredients

1/2 cup apple vinegar

1/2 cup roasted red bell peppers, chopped

1 tablespoon mustard

2 teaspoons garlic, minced

1/2 teaspoon salt

1/8 teaspoon ground black pepper

1/4 teaspoon smoked paprika

1 teaspoons lemon juice

1 cup olive oil

Whole grain pasta (package for 4 servings)

1/2 cup bell peppers, seeded and diced

½ cup cherry tomatoes, cut into halves

1/2 cup tofu parmesan

Directions

Prepare Vinaigrette dressing on the following way:

> Whisk (or blend) the vinegar, half of the peppers, mustard, garlic, salt, pepper, paprika and lemon juice in a food processor. Then, add the oil slowly at first, then a little faster to achieve fairly thick dressing.

Cut the remaining peppers into small strips. Add to the dressing. Adjust the seasonings.

Cook your favorite whole-grain pasta, rinse and drain. Combine pasta with dressing, peppers, and tomatoes, and toss well.

Refrigerate at least 1 hour. Toss gently before serving and divide among a serving plates. Sprinkle parmesan and serve chilled according to your taste.

Vegetable Herby Pizza

(Ready in about 35 minutes | Servings 4)

Ingredients

1 (14 ounce) package prebaked pizza crust

1 teaspoon oregano

1/4 cups broccoli florets

1 teaspoon basil

1/4 cups cauliflower florets

1 teaspoon rosemary

1 small red onion, sliced into rings

Dried red chili flakes, if desired

Salt to taste

1 cup vegan pizza cheese

Fresh black ground pepper to taste

Directions

Preheat the oven to 500 degrees F. Line a baking sheet with parchment paper.

Prepare pizza crust and place to the baking sheet. Layer broccoli and cauliflower florets, then layer the onion rings, and season with salt and pepper. Spread the pizza cheese and sprinkle herbs.

Bake about 15 minutes. If the cheese is not melted enough continue baking for a few minutes longer.

Let the pizza cool for a few minutes before cutting and serve immediately.

Chickpeas and Avocado Green Sandwiches

(Ready in about 20 minutes | Servings 5)

Ingredients

2 (15-ounce) cans peas chickpeas

2 tablespoons olive oil

1/4 teaspoon sea salt

1/4 teaspoon freshly ground black pepper

1/4 teaspoon red pepper flakes

10 slices bread

5 teaspoons vegan mayonnaise

2 green onion, sliced

1 red bell pepper, sliced

1/2 cup container alfalfa sprouts

2 avocados, pitted and thinly sliced

Directions

Rinse and drain the chickpeas. Mix the chickpeas, oil, salt, pepper and red pepper. Stir well to combine all ingredients and develop smooth puree.

Take bread slices and divide the chickpeas mixture among them. Spread mayonnaise evenly on the top. Then top with the onion, bell pepper, alfalfa sprouts, and avocado.

Top with the remaining bread slices and serve immediately.

Blueberries Pie Pizza

(Ready in about 45 minutes + 3 hours for pizza crust | Servings 8)

Ingredients

3 cups unbleached all-purpose flour

1 teaspoon salt

2 teaspoons instant yeast

1 ¼ cups warm water

2 tablespoons olive oil

2 tablespoons agave syrup

4 cups blueberries

2/3 cup granulated sugar

1/2 cup cool water

1/4 cup cornstarch

chocolate curls and chopped hazelnuts for garnish

Directions

To make the pizza dough, sift the flour, add salt and whisk well. Sprinkle the yeast and add the warm water, olive oil and agave syrup. Stir until everything is mixed well.

Cover the bowl with a fitted lid, and set aside in a warm place to rise for 3 hours.

Preheat the oven to 500 degrees F.

To prepare the topping, mix the blueberries, sugar, and 1/4 cup of the water in a large pan. Bring the mixture to a simmer without stirring.

Whisk together the cornstarch and the remaining water in a mixing bowl. Add the mixture into hot topping and simmer for 10 minutes.

Roll out the dough on floured surface.

Transfer the dough to a baking sheet, coated with parchment paper.

Bake for 15 minutes, till the pizza crust starts to brown. Set aside and allow the crust to cool to the room temperature.

Spread the blueberry mixture evenly over the cooled crust. Arrange with chocolate curls and chopped hazelnuts.

Party Mushroom Burgers

(Ready in about 1 hour | Servings 8)

Ingredients

3 teaspoons canola oil

1 medium onion, finely diced

1 teaspoon garlic, crushed

1 pound mushrooms, sliced

1/4 teaspoon dried basil

1/8 teaspoon dried rubbed sage

1/4 teaspoon salt

1/4 teaspoon black pepper

1 tablespoon soy sauce, preferably mushroom soy sauce

1/4 cup balsamic vinegar

1 1/2 cups cooked basmati rice

1 ½ cups cooked bulgur

1/4 cup soy flour

Directions

Heat 1 teaspoon of the canola oil in a wok or wide iron-skillet over medium-high heat. Add the onion, garlic, mushrooms, basil and sage. Cook until all of the liquid from mushrooms is evaporated. Add the mushroom soy sauce and vinegar and cook the mixture until it is dry.

Transfer the mushroom mixture in a mixing bowl and place in a fridge.

When the mushroom mixture is cool enough to handle, add the rice, bulgur, and flour. Season with salt and pepper. Stir to mix well. You can use a food processor to blend all ingredients easier.

Shape the mushroom mixture into 8 patties.

Heat 2 teaspoon of the oil in an iron-skillet over medium-high heat. Fry the patties for 4 to 5 minutes, on each side. Serve warm.

Chinese Ma-Po Tofu

(Ready in about 1 hour | Servings 4)

Ingredients

1/2 cup broccoli

1/2 cup cauliflower

3 tablespoons beans

2 tablespoons soy sauce

1 pound firm silken tofu, cubed

2 teaspoons vegetable oil

6 green onions, sliced

2 teaspoons garlic, crushed

1 dried chili

2 teaspoons fresh ginger, grated

2 teaspoons garlic paste

1 teaspoon sesame oil

Directions

Cut the broccoli and cauliflower into small florets. Blanch the florets for 10 minutes.

Soak the beans in 1 cup of boiling water for 10 minutes. Rinse and drain the beans, reserving 1/4 cup of the liquid. Chop the beans and set aside.

Pour 4 cups of water in a stockpot, and simmer the tofu for 3 to 4 minutes. Remove the tofu from the water carefully. Reserve.

In a wide skillet, heat the oil over medium-high flame. Stir-fry the onions, garlic, chili and ginger for a few minutes. Add the garlic paste and fry for 1 minute longer, stirring frequently.

Turn the flame to medium point. Add the prepared bean water and soy sauce to the skillet. Add the broccoli and cauliflower florets and stir-fry for 3 minutes.

If the sauce is too thick, add a few tablespoons of water. Add the tofu and sesame oil and stir to mix gently. Let the meal simmer for 2 minutes and serve warm.

Buns with Chewy Tempeh Bacon

(Ready in about 1 hour | Servings 6)

Ingredients

1 package (8 ounces) tempeh	Vegetable oil, for frying
1/4 cup soy sauce	6 whole-grain buns
3 tablespoons real maple syrup	Lettuce to taste
2 teaspoons liquid smoke	Salt to taste
1/4 cup water	Garlic mustard (optional)

Directions

Steam the whole block of tempeh for about 10 to 12 minutes.

Meanwhile, prepare the marinade in a mixing bowl. Combine soy sauce, maple syrup, liquid smoke, and water. Mix well.

Let the tempeh cool and cut it into bacon-size strips. Place slices in prepared marinade. Make sure all tempeh strips are coated and mix gently. Then let sit for 30 about minutes to mix the flavors.

Heat oil in a deep iron-skillet and fry the tempeh bacon strips over high flame, 5 minutes per side, or till they are chewy-crisp.

Remove from the oil and transfer to a large plate.

To make sandwiches: Cut the bun, layer salted lettuce leaves, place Tempeh Bacon and add mustard to taste. Arrange prepared sandwiches with additional lettuce leaves on a large platter.

Matchsticks and Cubes Party Salad

(Ready in about 20 minutes | Servings 2)

Ingredients

1 medium carrot

1 medium cucumber

1/2 cup cooked or canned bean sprouts

1 red bell pepper

1 small white onion

1 teaspoon apple cider vinegar

2 tablespoons extra-virgin olive oil

1/8 teaspoon chili pepper

1/4 teaspoon salt

1/8 teaspoon black pepper

1/2 teaspoon cumin

2 tablespoons alfalfa sprouts

½ cup firm tofu, cut into bite-sized cubes

Directions

Cut the vegetables into small matchsticks, as thin as possible. Place the vegetables matchsticks into large mixing bowl, add cooked bean sprouts, and toss to mix well. Add chili peppers.

Drizzle vinegar and oil and season with salt, pepper and cumin seeds. Sprinkle the alfalfa sprouts.

Top the salad with tofu cubes and serve immediately.

Mediterranean Pizza

(Ready in about 1 hour + 3 hours for dough | Servings 8)

Ingredients

2 cups white wheat flour

1 cup all-purpose flour

1 teaspoon salt

2 tablespoons sugar

2 teaspoons instant yeast, at room temperature

11/4 cups warm water (120°F)

2 tablespoons olive oil

6 tablespoons tomato sauce

2 tablespoons ketchup

1 cup non-diary mozzarella cheese, shredded

1 small handful fresh rosemary leaves

1 teaspoon oregano

1/2 yellow bell pepper, sliced

1/2 red bell pepper, sliced

1/2 small onion, sliced

1/2 cup pitted olives, sliced in half lengthwise

1/2 cup canned artichoke hearts, sliced in half

Directions

To prepare the pizza crust: Mix the flours, salt, and sugar in a large mixing bowl. Put the yeast on top of the dry mixture, then add the water and oil, and stir with the fork until all ingredients are combined well.

If the dough seems dry, add a little more water. Don't knead the dough. Cover the bowl with fitted lid, and let sit at the warm place to rise for about 3 hours.

Preheat the oven to 500 degrees F for 30 minutes.

Transfer the dough to floured surface. Roll out the dough as thin as possible.

Line a large baking sheet with parchment paper. Transfer prepared rolled-out dough to the backing sheet. Spread the tomato sauce and ketchup evenly on the pizza crust.

Then put the shredded cheese and top with the peppers, onion, olives, and artichokes. Sprinkle fresh rosemary and oregano.

Bake until the dough is crisp and cheese is golden, or about 15 minutes. Cut into squares and serve warm.

Chocolate-Cinnamon Sweet Pizza

(Ready in about 45 minutes | Servings 4)

Ingredients

1 cup dairy-free semisweet chocolate chips

1/3 cup sugar

2 tablespoons cocoa powder

1 teaspoon ground cinnamon

2 tablespoons vegan, non-hydrogenated margarine

2/3 cup powdered sugar

2/3 cup unbleached all-purpose flour

4 tablespoons (1/4 cup) vegan, non-hydrogenated margarine

1 (14 ounce) package prebaked pizza crust

Additional grated chocolate for garnish (optional)

Directions

Preheat the oven to 450 degrees F.

Combine the chocolate chips, sugar, cocoa powder, cinnamon, and melted margarine, and blend in a food processor.

To make the streusel, mix together the powdered sugar and flour in a small bowl. Add the remaining vegan melted margarine.

Spread the chocolate filling evenly on the pizza crust. Sprinkle the streusel evenly over the pizza.

Carefully place the pizza on a baking sheet.

Bake for 15 minutes, till the pizza crust is golden-brown and the streusel is melted.

Allow sweet pizza to cool for 15 minutes before cutting and serving. Sprinkle with grated chocolate and serve warmish.

Cauliflower-Almond Patties

(Ready in about 45 minutes | Servings 4)

Ingredients

2 cups fresh cauliflower florets	2 teaspoons fresh sage, chopped
1/2 cup sunflower sprouts	2 teaspoon extra-virgin olive oil
2 red onion, sliced	1/2 cup wheat germ
2 cloves garlic, minced	rye bread slices
1/2 cup vegan almond butter	1 tablespoon fresh parsley

Directions

Process the cauliflower, sprouts, onions, and garlic in an electric blender, till they are finely chopped.

In a medium bowl, mix prepared vegetable mixture with the almond butter and sage, till they are not too sticky. Shape the mixture into 4 patties.

Heat the oil in a wide heavy skillet over medium-high flame.

Dredge the patties in the wheat germ. Fry the patties shortly until they are crisp on each surface. Do not cook too long because they will become gooey.

Prepare rye bread slices. Divide patties among bread slices, sprinkle with parsley and serve immediately.

Sesame Romaine Salad

(Ready in about 15 minutes | Servings 6)

Ingredients

3 tablespoons toasted sesame oil

1 tablespoon tamari

1 tablespoon agave syrup

1/8 teaspoon Korean chili pepper

6 cups romaine

1 small onion, sliced

1/2 cup raisins

Directions

Make the dressing in first. Combine oil, tamari, agave syrup and chili pepper into a mixing bowl, cover and shake to mix well.

Chop the romaine into bite-sized pieces. Place romaine and onions in a large mixing bowl. Toss with dressing.

Divide salad in a glass serving bowls. Sprinkle raisins and serve.

Shiitake and Veggie Stir-Fry

(Ready in about 20 minutes | Servings 2)

Ingredients

2 medium onions, sliced

1 clove garlic, minced

1 red chili, sliced

1/2 cup bean sprouts, sliced

5-6 shiitake mushrooms, sliced

1/2 cup Napa cabbage, finely chopped

2 tablespoons olive oil

1/4 teaspoon sea salt

1/4 teaspoon freshly ground black pepper

2 teaspoons tamari sauce

1 teaspoon flaxseed oil

1 teaspoon flax seeds

Directions

In a deep mixing bowl, mix bean sprouts, mushrooms, and cabbage.

Heat the olive oil in a wide and deep saucepan. Sauté the onions, garlic and chili for 1 to 2 minutes, and then add the vegetable mix. Stir well to combine all ingredients.

Flip, toss or stir the vegetables in the saucepan as you want, in order to keep the vegetables moving. All ingredients have to fry equally. Add the salt and pepper.

When the vegetables start to soften, add the tamari sauce and flaxseed oil. Cook for 2 to 3 minutes.

Sprinkle flax seeds over stir-fry and serve warm.

Herby Roasted Potatoes in Wine

(Ready in about 1 hour | Servings 4)

Ingredients

2 cloves garlic, crushed

1/2 teaspoon ground black pepper

1 teaspoon salt

1 teaspoon dried rosemary

2 tablespoons dry white wine

1 tablespoon Dijon mustard

2 tablespoons olive oil

1 1/4 pounds baby Yukon potatoes, unpeeled and halved

2 medium green onions, finely sliced

2 tablespoons parsley

Lemon slices for garnish (optional)

Directions

Preheat the oven to 400 degrees F. Mix the garlic, pepper, salt, rosemary, wine, mustard and olive oil in a large mixing bowl.

Transfer prepared mixture in a glass casserole dish. Stir in the potatoes and green onions.

Cover with foil and bake for 30 minutes. Remove the foil and bake for 20 minutes longer, or until the potatoes are fork-tender. Sprinkle the chopped parsley, garnish with lemon slices and serve warm.

PART FOUR FAST SNACKS

Peanut Butter Crackers with Flax Seeds

(Ready in about 25 minutes | Servings 4)

Ingredients

1 tablespoon soy sauce

2 tablespoons canola oil

3 tablespoons vegan peanut butter

1/4 cup brown rice flour

1/3 cup whole wheat flour

3 tablespoons cornstarch

1 teaspoon baking soda

1 teaspoon sea salt

1 tablespoon flax seeds

1/4 cup soy milk

Directions

Preheat the oven to 350 degrees F. Line a baking sheets with parchment baking paper.

Whisk soy sauce, oil and peanut butter.

To make a dough, combine together wet ingredients with the flours, cornstarch and baking soda, and season with salt. Add flax seeds and the soy non-diary milk, a little at a time. Mix all ingredients well.

Roll out the dough, and then cut out shapes with cookie cutter. Repeat till you run out of dough

Bake for 13 minutes, until the crackers are golden-brown. Let cool prepared crackers.

Serve with your favorite vegan sauce or vegan sour cream.

Pita bread with Hummus and Salad

(Ready in about 25 minutes | Servings 6)

Ingredients

1 red onion, finely chopped

2 cloves garlic, minced

1 tablespoon canola oil

1/4 cup tahini

2 tablespoon lemon juice

1 teaspoon lemon zest

2 cups edamame, cooked

1/2 teaspoon salt

Black pepper to taste

6 small pita breads

1 cucumber for garnish

1 large tomato (optional)

Cayenne pepper to taste

Directions

To make Hummus, heat the oil in a saucepan. Sauté the onion and garlic, until the onion is tender and translucent.

Place edamame, onion, garlic, tahini, lemon juice, lemon zest salt and pepper in a blender and buzz a few times until well-combined.

Adjust seasonings. Cut cucumber and tomato into thin slices, season with salt and use for garnish.

Place pita breads on a serving plate, add hummus, sprinkle cayenne pepper and garnish with salad of choice.

Baked Crispy Kale Chips

(Ready in about 40 minutes | Servings 4)

Ingredients

1 ½ cups kale, chopped into small pieces

2 tablespoons olive oil

1 tablespoon balsamic vinegar

1 tablespoon nutritional yeast

1/2 teaspoon kosher salt

Directions

Preheat the oven to 350 degrees F. Prepare the baking sheets with parchment paper.

Combine the kale pieces with the oil, vinegar, yeast, and salt in a large mixing bowl.

Transfer prepared kale to the baking sheets and bake for 30 minutes, until the kale chips is crisp.

Juicy Couscous with Fruit and Almonds

(Ready in about 40 minutes | Servings 4)

Ingredients

1 lb. couscous

1/ ½ cups vegetable stock

1/2 cup dried apricots

1/4 cup figs, pitted and roughly chopped

1/4 cup cranberries

1/4 cup grains

1/2 teaspoon salt

1/4 teaspoon freshly ground black pepper

2 tablespoons olive oil

2 tablespoons lime juice

2 cups canned chickpeas

fresh mint leaves to taste

handful of cilantro (optional)

3/4 cup almonds

Directions

Preheat the oven to 400 degrees F.

Combine stock, apricots, figs and cranberries in a wide and deep saucepan, and bring to a boil.

Pour the prepared hot stock over the couscous in an ovenproof dish.

Cover the grains with warm water to improve their absorption of minerals. Set aside for 15 minutes.

Fluff up the couscous with a fork and add salt and pepper. Drizzle the oil and lime juice. To prepare chickpeas, drain and rinse them under cold water. Then add the chickpeas to couscous. Mix the ingredients well.

Bake the couscous for 15 minutes. Fluff up the grains, and add the mint and cilantro.

Stir-fry the almonds in a heavy frying pan over moderate heat, stirring constantly for 5 minutes. Sprinkle the almonds over the prepared couscous with fruits and serve warm.

White Bean Spread

(Ready in about 20 minutes | Servings 4)

Ingredients

2 cups cooked white beans	2 tablespoons olive oil
1 teaspoon oil	1 tablespoon fresh basil
2 small green onions, sliced	1/2 teaspoon salt
4 cloves garlic, sliced	1/4 teaspoon freshly ground black pepper
1 tablespoon lemon juice	Crackers (optional)
1 teaspoon lemon zest	Cumin to taste

Directions

Rinse and drain the beans. Purée the beans in a blender.

Pour the oil in a skillet over high heat. Add the onions and garlic, stirring constantly until the onions develop a light golden color.

Add the prepared onions and garlic to the puréed beans in the blender. Add lemon juice, lemon zest and olive oil. Add basil, and season with salt and pepper. Adjust the thickness of the prepared mixture with just a little water.

Serve with your favorite crackers and sprinkle cumin for garnish.

Italian Sesame Salty Cookies

(Ready in about 40 minutes | Servings 4)

Ingredients

2 tablespoons nutritional yeast

1/4 cups oats

1/4 teaspoon Italian seasoning

1 teaspoons baking powder

1 tablespoon white miso

4 tablespoons vegan margarine

1 tablespoon canola oil

3 tablespoons non-dairy milk

1 clove garlic, finely minced

1 tablespoon toasted sesame seeds

1¼ cups whole wheat pastry flour

Directions

Preheat the oven to 350 degrees F. Prepare baking sheet with parchment paper.

Combine the nutritional yeast, Italian seasoning, miso, oil and garlic in a mixing bowl. Mix well and reserve.

Whisk together the flour, oats and baking powder in a large mixing bowl. Add the margarine and mix all ingredients together. Add the milk, a little at a time and add sesame seeds.

Divide the dough into equal pieces. Press down as flat the cookies.

Bake for 15 minutes, or until the cookies are golden and crispy. Remove to a wire rack to cool.

Croutons with Mushroom Pâté

(Ready in about 20 minutes | Servings 6)

Ingredients

Non-stick cooking spray

1 tablespoon canola oil

1 cup mushrooms, sliced

1 cup onion, chopped

1 cup scallions, chopped

1 cup firm tofu

3 tablespoons chopped fresh parsley

1 tablespoon paprika

1 tablespoon cornstarch

1/2 teaspoon salt

1/4 teaspoon freshly ground black pepper

10 black olives

Croutons of choice

Directions

Preheat the oven to 400 degrees F.

Prepare a standard loaf pan with non-stick spray.

Preheat the canola oil in a wide saucepan over medium-low flame. Add the mushrooms, onion, and scallions and cook for 10 to 15 minutes.

Transfer the vegetables to an electric blender. Add the tofu, parsley, paprika, cornstarch, salt and black pepper. Blend ingredients until they are smooth.

Transfer the mixture into the loaf pan and bake for 30 minutes.

Let cool in the fridge for several hours. Garnish with olives.

Serve chilled with your favorite croutons.

Italian Caponata with Nuts

(Ready in about 50 minutes | Servings 4)

Ingredients

2 cups eggplant, cut into bite-sized cubes

1 tablespoon brown sugar

3 tablespoons olive oil

1 ½ cups tomatoes, diced

2 stalks celery, finely chopped

8 pitted kalamata olives

1 medium red onion, chopped

1 tablespoon pine nuts, toasted

3 cloves garlic, chopped

1/2 teaspoon fine sea salt

1/3 cup red wine vinegar

1/8 teaspoon freshly ground black pepper

2 tablespoons red wine

1 tablespoon fresh basil, chopped

Directions

Salt the eggplant cubes and place them in a colander. Let it stand to drain for 30 minutes. After that, rinse the eggplant cubes under water and pat dry.

Heat 2 tablespoons of the olive oil in a large saucepan over medium-high flame. Add the celery, onion, and garlic and sauté until the onion is tender. Set aside.

Heat the remaining 1 tablespoon of the oil in the pan over medium-high flame. Add the eggplant cubes and cook until they are slightly tender, about 8 minutes.

Add the cooked eggplant cubes to the bowl with the onions and celery.

To prepare the sauce: Add the vinegar, wine and sugar to the saucepan, bring to a boil, and reduce the mixture in half by the liquid is evaporated.

Pour the sauce over the eggplant mixture and stir till the vegetables are well coated.

When the mixture is still warm, add the tomatoes, olives and pine nuts. Season with salt and pepper and taste.

Let the prepared Caponata stand for 30 minutes in order to serve chilled. Sprinkle chopped basil and serve with toasted bread.

Cold Artichoke Dip

(Ready in about 25 minutes | Servings 6)

Ingredients

1/2 cup sliced almonds

2 cloves garlic, minced

1 2/3 cup canned artichoke hearts

1 onion, diced

2/3 cup soy mayonnaise

2 tablespoons fresh dill

1 tablespoon fresh basil

1/2 teaspoon Sea salt

1/4 red pepper flakes

Fresh rosemary for garnish

Directions

Process the almonds in an electric blender. Add the garlic, pulse a few times till your mixture are well blended.

Drain the artichoke hearts. Add the artichoke hearts to the almond mixture and pulse till coarsely chopped.

Add the onions, mayonnaise, dill, basil, and mix well.

Season with sea salt and pepper flakes. Serve chilled with toasted bread and garnish with fresh rosemary.

Roasted Tomatoes with Cashew Ricotta

(Ready in about 25 minutes | Servings 6)

Ingredients

1/2 cup raw cashew

freshly squeezed juice from 1 lemon

2 tablespoons olive oil

2 cloves roasted garlic

1 pound tofu

1 teaspoons dried basil

1 teaspoon salt

12 small Roasted tomatoes

Directions

Drain and crumble the tofu.

Process together the cashews, lemon juice, olive oil and garlic in an electric blender. Blend until ingredients develop creamy paste form.

Then add the crumbled tofu, basil and salt to the paste and blend well.

Arrange with roasted tomatoes and serve as a cold appetizer or snack.

Movie Night Popcorn

(Ready in about 20 minutes | Servings 2)

Ingredients

1 cup corn kernels

3 tablespoons cooking oil

1/2 teaspoon smoked paprika

2 teaspoon salt

1 teaspoon red pepper flakes

1/2 teaspoon garlic powder

1 teaspoon ground cumin

1/4 teaspoon cayenne pepper

Directions

In a heavy dip pot, heat the cooking oil over high-medium flame. Add 1 kernel of popcorn. When the kernel pops, add all corn kernels.

Cover and make popcorns by shaking your pot to move kernels around inside.

Replace the popcorn in a large bowl.

Mix together smoked paprika, salt, pepper flakes, garlic powder, cumin, cayenne pepper and stir to combine all spices.

Sprinkle spice mix over popcorn, toss and enjoy your movie night!

Festive Vegetable Appetizer

(Ready in about 1 hour 25 minutes | Servings 4)

Ingredients

2 medium leeks

2 teaspoons salt

2 cups green beans

1 large zucchini

1 large yellow squash

1/2 cup vegetable oil

1 cup mushrooms

Salt to taste

Freshly ground black pepper to taste

1/4 cup fresh tarragon, chopped

1 cup Tomato paste

Garlic for garnish, crushed

Parsley for garnish, chopped

Directions

Preheat the oven to 375 degrees F.

Wash all vegetables under water. Cut the leeks into halves lengthwise.

Carefully put the leeks into a stockpot and add enough water to cover the leeks. Add 1 teaspoon of salt. Bring the stockpot of the water to a boil over high heat. Reduce the heat and simmer the leeks until they are tender. Drain the leeks and rinse under cold water. When the leeks are cool enough to handle, remove the root end and separate the leaves. Reserve.

In the stockpot, bring water with 1 teaspoon of salt to boil. Add the green beans and blanch them for a few minutes. Remove the beans from the stockpot and rinse under running cold water. Set aside.

Cut the zucchini and yellow squash lengthwise into strips. Brush the strips with vegetable oil. Season with salt and pepper to taste.

Transfer the vegetable strips on a baking sheet with parchment paper. Roast the vegetables for 10 minutes. Flip the vegetables and roast the other side until tender.

Meanwhile, roast the mushrooms for 15 minutes or until they are tender.

Coat a loaf pan with a small amount of nonstick spray. Place the leeks and bake until they are soft and crisp. Sprinkle with tarragon.

Layer leeks, zucchini, yellow squash, and mushrooms. Add the remaining vegetable oil and cover with waxed paper and then with aluminum foil.

Bake for about 40 minutes. Remove from the oven and let it cool. Garnish with tomato paste, garlic and parsley.

Rustic Baked Apples

(Ready in about 30 minutes | Servings 4)

Ingredients

3 1/3 cups apples, peeled and sliced into a little less than

1/4 cup brown sugar

1 teaspoon ground cinnamon

1/4 teaspoon ground nutmeg

2 teaspoons toasted ground walnuts

Directions

Preheat the oven to 350 degrees F.

Prepare a cookie sheet with parchment paper.

Cut the apples into thin bite-sized slices. Place the apple slices on the cookie sheet.

Sprinkle with the sugar, cinnamon and nutmeg. Cover the apples with aluminum foil, and bake 15 minutes.

Then flip the apples, sprinkle the walnuts and bake uncovered for 5 minutes more. You can serve with your favorite waffles.

Party Vegan Balls

(Ready in about 1 hour 25 minutes | Servings 6)

Ingredients

2 cups masa harina flour	1/4 teaspoon cinnamon
1/2 cup vegetable oil	1 avocado, sliced
1 cup water	2 canned chipotle peppers
1/3 cup vegan sour cream	1/2 teaspoon salt
1/2 cup corn	1/4 teaspoon black pepper
1/2 cup black beans	1/4 teaspoon cayenne peppers

Directions

Preheat the oven to 400 degrees F.

Prepare a baking sheet by lining it with a silicone baking sheet (e.g. Silpat) or parchment baking paper.

In a large mixing bowl, combine flour, oil, water, sour cream, corn, beans, cinnamon, avocado slices and peppers. Season with salt, pepper and cayenne.

Take 2 tablespoons of the mixture and shape it into a ball. Repeat this procedure with the remaining mixture. Place prepared balls on the baking sheet.

Bake for 15 to 20 minutes and then transfer to a large serving platter.

Blueberry Sauce with Cinnamon Cream Spread

(Ready in about 1 hour | Servings 4)

Ingredients

1/3 cup agave nectar

2 teaspoons grated ginger

1 cup fresh blueberries

1/2 cup vegan non-dairy cream cheese

1/2 teaspoon ground cinnamon

1/2 teaspoon nutmeg, grated

Directions

To prepare the blueberry sauce: Put agave nectar, ginger and blueberries in a wide saucepan.

Bring the sauce to a low boil, cover with a lid and reduce the heat to low temperature. Simmer for 10 minutes.

To prepare the cream spread: Combine non-diary cream cheese, cinnamon and grated nutmeg.

Transfer to the refrigerator. Serve this snack chilled. Garnish with fresh blueberries.

Red Hot Spread

(Ready in about 20 minutes | Servings 4)

Ingredients

1/3 cup bread crumbs

2 cups roasted bell pepper, drained

1 clove garlic, minced

1 teaspoon sesame oil

Juice from 1 lemon

1 teaspoon cumin

1/4 cup tahini

1/2 teaspoon salt

1/4 teaspoon red pepper flakes

Freshly ground black pepper (optional)

Directions

Place bread crumbs, peppers, garlic, sesame oil, lemon juice, cumin and tahini in a food processor or an electric blender.

Blend and process until just smooth. Season with salt and pepper.

Sprinkle red pepper flakes and serve chilled with your favorite vegetable sticks.

Spinach Tofu Spread

(Ready in about 30 minutes | Servings 8)

Ingredients

1 ½ cups soft tofu

2 cups spinach leaves

2 cloves garlic

1 tablespoon lemon juice

1 teaspoon fine sea salt

1 teaspoon dried basil

1/4 cup nutritional yeast

1/4 cup tahini

2 teaspoons white miso

Croutons for garnish.

Directions

To prepare tofu: Bring a pot of water to a boil, add tofu and simmer for 5 minutes. Drain well and set aside.

Bring a large stockpot of water to a boil over high-medium flame and blanch the spinach leaves. Cook for 1 to 2 minutes, until the water develops bright green color. Drain the spinach leaves and squeeze the spinach leaves to remove all excess water.

Place the spinach, garlic and lemon juice in a wide and deep saucepan. Season with salt and basil. Cook over medium heat for 3 minutes.

Transfer to a blender or a food processor and pulse a few times. Add the prepared tofu, yeast, tahini and miso, and process until the mixture is smooth.

Replace to a large serving bowl, garnish with your favorite croutons and serve chilled.

Herby Homemade Croutons

(Ready in about 25 minutes | Servings 8)

Ingredients

4 cups bread bite-sized cubes

2 tablespoons extra-virgin olive oil

1/2 teaspoon dried basil

1/2 teaspoon dried oregano

1/2 teaspoon dried rosemary

1 teaspoon spices for Tzatziki

1/4 teaspoon onion powder

1/4 teaspoon cayenne pepper

Directions

Cut your favorite vegan bread into bite-sized cubes. Drizzle the bread cubes with extra-virgin olive oil.

To make herb mixture: Place basil, oregano, rosemary, tzatziki, onion powder and cayenne in a mixing bowl and mix well to combine.

Sprinkle the herb mixture over the cubes and coat them evenly.

Preheat the oven to 300 degrees F. Layer the cubes of bread to a single layer on a non-stick baking sheet and bake for about 15 minutes.

Let it cool and serve with your favorite vegan spread or vegan pâté. You can garnish with vegan sour cream and herbs of choice, too.

Salsa Fresca with Tortilla Chips

(Ready in about 20 minutes | Servings 14)

Ingredients

2 cups tomatoes, diced

1 cup red onion, sliced

1 cup white onion, sliced

1 cup fresh cilantro leaves, chopped

1 cup corn kernels

1/4 cup lemon juice

2 jalapeño peppers, minced

2 tablespoons garlic, minced

1/2 teaspoon sea salt

1/4 teaspoon red pepper flakes

1/2 teaspoon dried basil

1/2 teaspoon dried oregano

Rosemary for garnish

Tortilla chips of choice

Directions

Combine tomatoes, onions, cilantro, corn kernels, lemon juice, jalapeño and garlic in a large mixing bowl. Add salt, pepper flakes, basil, and oregano.

Taste and adjust the seasonings. Keep Salsa refrigerated.

Garnish with rosemary and serve with your favorite tortilla chips.

Club Sandwiches with Avocado Spread

(Ready in about 20 minutes | Servings 8)

Ingredients

Flesh of 2 avocados

1 cup raw cashews

1/2 cup onion, diced

1 jalapeño pepper, seeded and minced

1/2 teaspoon fine sea salt

1/4 teaspoon freshly ground black pepper

1/4 teaspoon tarragon

Bread slices of choice

Directions

Combine avocados, cashews, onion and jalapeño in a bowl of your food processor or an electric blender. Add salt, pepper, and tarragon.

Purée until your mixture is very smooth.

Make club sandwiches and place on a large serving platter. Garnish with additional herbs to taste and serve as a cool appetizer or a great party snack.

Spiced Squash Hummus with Chips

(Ready in about 1 hour | Servings 8)

Ingredients

2 cups roasted butternut squash, chopped

1 can cooked garbanzo beans

1 tablespoon olive oil

1/4 cup tahini

Juice from fresh lemon

1 tablespoon curry powder

1 teaspoon garlic powder

1 teaspoon ground cumin

1/2 teaspoon sea salt

1/4 teaspoon freshly ground black pepper

Vegan chips of choice

Directions

To prepare the squash: Cut the squash into 8 pieces, drizzle with the olive oil, sprinkle salt and pepper. Preheated oven to 400 degrees F. Bake squash pieces for 45 minutes.

Rinse and drain cooked garbanzo beans.

Place roasted squash, beans, tahini, lemon, curry, garlic powder, cumin, salt and pepper in an electric blender or a food processor. Blend until the hummus is smooth.

Serve chilled with your favorite chips.

Mini Pita Bread with Cauliflower Hummus

(Ready in about 25 minutes | Servings 6)

Ingredients

1 cup steamed cauliflower, chopped

1 can cooked garbanzo beans, drained and rinsed

1½ tablespoons lemon juice

1 teaspoon orange zest

2 tablespoons olive oil

3 tablespoons tahini

2 teaspoons sesame oil

1 teaspoon salt

1/4 teaspoon ground black pepper

Pita bread of choice

Directions

Combine cauliflower, garbanzo beans, lemon, orange zest, olive oil, tahini, and sesame oil. Season with salt and pepper.

Process all ingredients in a food processor and blend until the mixture is well smooth, scraping the sides with a rubber spatula.

Cut pita bread into small pieces and serve with the chilled cauliflower hummus.

Mashed eggplant with Crackers – Baba Ghanoush

(Ready in about 1 hour | Servings 6)

Ingredients

1 eggplant

Juice from 1 fresh lemon

1/4 cup tahini

3 tablespoons fresh parsley

1 tablespoon garlic, minced

1 teaspoon garlic powder

1/2 teaspoon salt

1/4 teaspoon Black pepper

1/4 smoked paprika

Toasted sesame oil (optional)

Crackers of choice

Toasted sesame seeds (optional)

Directions

Preheat the oven to 375 degrees F.

Drill the small holes all over the eggplant with a fork. Put the eggplant in the oven, on the rack, and roast for about 45 minutes.

Remove from the oven and allow to stand for about 15 minutes to cool.

Peel the eggplant and reserve the flesh.

Add the lemon juice, tahini, parsley, garlic, garlic powder, salt, pepper, and paprika. Add sesame seeds if you want. Place in a blender and purée until the mixture is smooth.

Drizzle the sesame oil on top and serve with your favorite crackers.

Butter Bean Dip with Veggie Sticks

(Ready in about 20 minutes | Servings 8)

Ingredients

1½ cups canned butter beans

1 cup leeks

2 cloves garlic, minced

1 tablespoon apple cider vinegar

1/2 teaspoon ground cumin

1/2 cup vegetable oil

1/2 teaspoon fine kosher salt

1/4 teaspoon black pepper

1/4 teaspoon paprika

Parsley for garnish

Veggie sticks of choice

Directions

To prepare beans: Drain and Rinse under cold water.

Combine beans, leeks, garlic, vinegar, cumin, vegetable oil, salt, black pepper and paprika in a bowl of a food processor.

Blend all ingredients until they are smooth.

Sprinkle the parsley and serve with your favorite veggie sticks.

Mini pancakes with Mushroom Filling (Blini)

(Ready in about 40 minutes | Servings 4)

Ingredients

1/2 cup cornmeal

1/2 cup wheat pastry flour

1 teaspoons baking powder

1 teaspoon baking soda

1/4 teaspoon cayenne pepper

1/4 teaspoon ground cumin

1/4 teaspoon sea salt

1/4 cup yellow corn, fresh

2 tablespoon olive oil

1/2 cup non-diary milk

1 ¼ teaspoons cider vinegar

2 tablespoons water

2 tablespoons onions, sliced

1/2 cup mushrooms

1 large red pepper, seeded

1 clove garlic, minced

Directions

Combine the cornmeal, flour, baking powder, baking soda, cayenne, cumin, and salt together in a mixing bowl. Chop the corn with a kitchen knife.

Mix the corn kernels, olive oil, milk, vinegar, and 2 tablespoons of water.

Combine the wet and dry mixture and stir to mix well. Stir in the onions.

Heat your mini pancake pan over medium heat and add a little bit oil. Evenly distribute the oil over the pan. Cook a blini for 2 minutes or until bubbles appear around the outer edge and blini has golden-brown color.

Repeat that process with the other side of the blini.

Transfer the blini on a serving platter.

To make mushroom filling: Cut the mushrooms into thin slices. Cut the pepper into thin strips. Chop the onions.

Heat remaining teaspoon of olive oil in another skillet. Add the onions, garlic and mushrooms. Sauté the vegetables for 4 minutes. Add the peppers to the skillet and cook until the vegetables are mostly dry.

Place a small amount of the mushroom filling on warm blini and serve warm.

Stuffed Poblano Peppers

(Ready in about 40 minutes | Servings 6)

Ingredients

6 poblano peppers

1/2 cup almonds

1 clove garlic, minced

1 tablespoon nutritional yeast

3/4 cup mashed potatoes

1/4 teaspoon sea salt

1/8 teaspoon black pepper

Oil to taste

Tomato Sauce, for garnish

Directions

Preheat the oven to 350 degrees F.

Cook poblano peppers in a pot of boiling salted water for 5 minutes, until they are soft.

Drain and rinse under water. Cut a slit down the length of each pepper. Cut the seeds and pith from the peppers carefully.

Process the almonds in a spice mill.

To make almond filling: Mix the garlic, yeast, and potatoes, and add grinded almonds. Season with salt and black pepper.

Fill each pepper with the almond filling. Place your filled peppers in an ovenproof dish. Brush the top of each pepper with oil to taste.

Bake your dish for 25 minutes. Pour Tomato Sauce over peppers and serve warm.

Bruschetta with Sun-Dried Tomato and Mushrooms

(Ready in about 30 minutes | Servings 6)

Ingredients

1 loaf bread of choice

2 cloves garlic, peeled

4 tablespoons extra-virgin olive oil

1 cup mushrooms of choice

Fine sea salt to taste

Freshly ground black pepper to taste

2 tablespoons Sun-Dried Tomato Pesto

rosemary, for garnish

Olives, for garnish

Directions

Cut the bread into slices, as thin as possible. Cut 12 slices and set aside.

Cut a garlic clove in half lengthwise. Rub the garlic on the bread slices. Brush a little oil on the bread slices.

To make bruschetta, heat non-stick pan. Place the bruschetta and fry until they are brown. Repeat this process until all bruschetta are baked. Set aside.

Brush the mushrooms with olive oil. Season the mushrooms with salt and pepper.

Saute the mushrooms in a saucepan over medium flame, stirring occasionally. Set aside.

When the mushrooms are cool enough, slice them into very thin strips.

Spread 1/2 teaspoon of tomato pesto over the garlic side of each bruschetta. Add mushrooms mixture and sprinkle rosemary for garnish. Cut olives lengthwise and place on top of bruschetta.

Transfer the bruschetta on a large serving platter, garnish with additional rosemary and olives and serve.

Veggie Sticks and Chips in Piquant Dip

(Ready in about 20 minutes | Servings 6)

Ingredients

3/4 cup plain non-dairy yogurt

3 tablespoons capers

2 tablespoons fresh dill, chopped

2 tablespoons chopped chives

2 tablespoons lemon juice

1/2 teaspoon salt

1/4 teaspoon freshly ground black pepper

veggie sticks of choice, for garnish

chips of choice, for garnish

Directions

Combine yogurt, capers, dill, chives and lemon juice in a small mixing bowl.

Season with salt and pepper, taste and adjust the seasonings.

Keep chilled until it is ready to serve. Garnish with veggie sticks and favorite chips and serve.

Chili Roasted Nuts

(Ready in about 25 minutes | Servings 8)

Ingredients

1 cup unsalted raw peanuts

1/2 cup walnuts

1 tablespoon peanut oil

1 teaspoon brown sugar

2 teaspoons fine sea salt

1/2 teaspoon freshly ground black pepper

2 teaspoons chili powder

1 teaspoon cayenne pepper

1 teaspoon ground cumin

3/4 teaspoon unsweetened cocoa powder

Directions

Preheat the oven to 350 degrees F. Prepare a large baking sheet and set aside.

Combine the peanuts, walnuts, peanut oil, sugar, and 1 teaspoon of salt. Spread the nuts evenly on the baking sheet, and bake, stirring the nuts occasionally.

Bake for a 20 minutes, until the nuts are browned and they are fragrant.

Meanwhile, mix the remaining 1 teaspoon of salt, black pepper, chili powder, cayenne pepper, cumin and cocoa powder in a mixing bowl. Stir to combine all ingredients well.

Remove the nuts from the oven. Stir prepared mixture into the peanuts and walnuts. Let cool and keep in dry and cool place.

Pinto Bean Dip

(Ready in about 20 minutes | Servings 10)

Ingredients

2 cups cooked pinto beans

2 teaspoons olive oil

1 medium white onion, finely chopped

1 jalapeno, minced

1/2 teaspoon ground cumin

1/2 teaspoon chili powder

1/2 teaspoon garlic powder

1 medium yellow bell pepper, sliced

1 medium green bell pepper, sliced

1 tablespoon apple vinegar

1/2 teaspoon kosher salt

1/4 teaspoon red pepper flakes

1 sprig rosemary for garnish

Directions

Rinse and drain the beans. Mash the beans in a food processor, until the mixture is smooth. Reserve.

Heat the oil in a heavy skillet over medium-high flame. Sauté the onion, and fresh jalapeño just until the onion starts to soften. Add the cumin, chili powder and garlic powder. Cook until the spices are fragrant and the onion is translucent and tender.

Add the peppers, stirring occasionally. When the peppers are hot, reduce the heat to low, add the beans to the pan, and stir to mix well.

Add the vinegar and adjust the consistency with a little water. Cook for 10 minutes longer.

Season with salt and pepper flakes. Garnish with rosemary and serve fresh.

Classic Basic Bruschetta

(Ready in about 20 minutes | Servings 7)

Ingredients

14 slices French baguette bread

2 cloves garlic

4 medium tomatoes, chopped

2 tablespoons extra-virgin olive oil

1/4 teaspoon salt

1 teaspoon dried oregano

1 teaspoon dried basil

2 tablespoons fresh basil leaves, for garnish

Directions

To make spread: Mix tomatoes, oil, salt, oregano and basil in a bowl. Cover and let marinate about 2 hours.

Meanwhile, cut baguette into thin slices, as thin as possible. Toast bread slices. Cut garlic cloves in halves lengthwise.

Rub the cut side of the garlic clove over the toasted bread slices.

Place marinated tomato spread on bread slices and transfer the bruschetta on a large serving platter. Garnish with chopped basil leaves and serve right away.

Fresh Party Guacamole

(Ready in about 25 minutes | Servings 12)

Ingredients

4 ripe avocados

2 tablespoons lemon juice

1 tablespoon orange zest

2 cloves garlic, minced

4 green onions, thinly sliced

1 small pickled jalapeño, minced

1 tablespoon cilantro, chopped

1/2 teaspoon kosher salt

1/4 teaspoon black pepper, ground

2 tablespoons soy mayonnaise

Directions

Mash the avocados in a mixing bowl.

Add the rest of the ingredients: lemon juice, orange zest, garlic, onions, jalapeño, and cilantro. Add soy mayonnaise.

Muddle the ingredients until they are well combined.

Season with salt and pepper. Taste and adjust the seasonings.

Club Sandwiches with Smoky Cheese

(Ready in about 45 minutes | Servings 16)

Ingredients

2 cups non-dairy milk

1/4 cup agar flakes

1/2 cup almonds

1/2 cup nutritional yeast

2 tablespoons white miso

2 tablespoons soy sauce

1 tablespoon liquid smoke

1 tablespoon onion powder

1 tablespoon garlic powder

1 tablespoon ground mustard seed

1/2 teaspoon salt

1/2 teaspoon smoked paprika

1 tablespoon alfalfa sprouts

1 teaspoon ground black pepper

Bread slices

Directions

Prepare a non-stick loaf pan.

Place the milk and agar flakes in a stockpot and bring to a boil.

In the meantime, place the almonds, yeast, miso, soy sauce, liquid smoke, onion powder, garlic powder, mustard seed, salt, paprika, alfalfa sprouts and pepper in a food processor and purée until smooth.

To make vegan non-diary smoky cheese: Add the blended mixture in the milk and agar and stir to combine all ingredients. Cook over medium heat a few minutes.

Transfer into the loaf pan and bake for 15 minutes.

Keep in a fridge. Make the club sandwiches and serve as a party snack or cold appetizer.

Vegan BBQ – Tofu and Vegetable Skewers

(Ready in about 1 hour 30 minutes | Servings 4)

Ingredients

1 (14-ounce) package extra-firm tofu

8 mushrooms, chopped in half

1 green bell pepper, chopped into chunks

1 red bell pepper

1 yellow bell pepper

1 zucchini, chopped

3/4 cup vegan marinade

skewers, pre-soaked

1/2 teaspoon fine salt

1/4 freshly ground black pepper

1 teaspoon cayenne pepper

Directions

Drain and press the tofu first. Cut prepared tofu into bite-sized cubes.

To prepare veggies: Cut the mushrooms in halves, cut peppers and zucchini into bite-sized chunks.

Combine tofu and veggies in a mixing bowl. Pour a vegan marinade over tofu chunks and allow to marinate for at least one hour.

Carefully slide tofu and veggies onto skewers. Season with salt, pepper and cayenne pepper. Adjust the seasonings.

Place on your indoor grill or a barbecue and grill for 5 to 6 minutes on each side.

Transfer to the serving platter and serve alongside your favorite vegan sauce.

Yalanci Dolmas with Non-dairy Yogurt

(Ready in about 30 minutes | Servings 6)

Ingredients

2 cups brown rice, cooked

2 tablespoons mint leaves, finely chopped

2 tablespoons apple cider vinegar

2 tablespoons lemon juice

2 tablespoons canola oil

1/2 cup hazelnuts, finely chopped

1/2 teaspoon salt

1/4 black pepper

1/8 teaspoon cinnamon

12 grape leaves

Non-dairy yogurt for serving

Lemon slices for garnish

Directions

Combine the rice, mint, vinegar, lemon juice, oil, hazelnuts, salt, pepper and cinnamon and mix in a large bowl until all ingredients are well combined.

Prepare grape leaves. Place 2 tablespoons of prepared mixture in the center of the leaf, and wrap up like a burrito. Repeat with all leaves.

Garnish with lemon slices. Serve with non-dairy yogurt, warm or cold, as a perfect appetizer.

Crispy Onion-Garlic Croustades

(Ready in about 1 hour | Servings 8)

Ingredients

8 slices bread without crusts

2 tablespoons olive oil

3 medium leeks

2 garlic cloves, crushed

1 tablespoon brown sugar, softened

1/2 teaspoon salt

1/2 teaspoon freshly ground black pepper

handful of fresh basil, chopped

Directions

Preheat the oven to 325 degrees F. Grease 8 tart pans.

To make croustades: Flatten the slices of bread with a rolling pin. Brush both sides of slices with olive oil. Press the bread slices into the patty pans.

Bake for 40 minutes, until they are crisp and fragrant.

Chop the leeks into long strips, as thin as possible.

Heat olive oil in a skillet, and sauté the leeks and garlic, until the leeks are tender. Season with salt and pepper and adjust the seasonings.

Add the sugar, cover, and sauté for another 10 minutes, or until the leeks have caramelized.

Place 1 tablespoon of the caramelized onions on the crispy croustades and return to the oven for 5 minutes.

Garnish with fresh basil leaves and serve warm.

Mediterranean Tomato Galette

(Ready in about 40 minutes | Servings 8)

Ingredients

1 ¾ cups fine pastry flour

1/2 teaspoon salt

1 teaspoon brown sugar

1/3 cup olive oil

3 tablespoons cold water

5 medium tomatoes

2 cloves garlic, minced

1 teaspoon fresh rosemary

1/2 cup vegan non-diary Parmesan

Olives of choice

Directions

To make pie pastry: Put flour, salt and sugar in a large mixing bowl. Create a hole in the center and fill it with oil and water. Whisk with fork to make a bit wet, sticky dough. Allow to rest 10 minutes.

Stretch and roll the dough out to a 12-inch size on a floured surface. Then prick the whole surface of the pastry with a fork.

Preheat oven to 400 degrees F. Prepare a large baking sheet with parchment paper.

To make tomato filling: Cut tomatoes into small and thin slices. Add garlic and rosemary. Season with salt and pepper.

Place the tomato filling in the middle of the pastry and fold over edges. Scatter the Parmesan in the center of the pastry. Place olives on top if desired.

Bake for 45 minutes, cool for a few minutes and serve.

Mini-Toast with Broad Beans

(Ready in about 35 minutes | Servings 12)

Ingredients

1 lb. fresh broad beans

1 onion, chopped

3 tablespoons olive oil

sea salt to taste

freshly ground black pepper to taste

2 tablespoons coriander, roughly chopped

1 teaspoon smoked paprika

1/2 teaspoon cayenne pepper

2 tablespoons apple cider vinegar

1 tablespoon orange zest

Mini toasted bread slices of choice

Parsley for garnish

Directions

Shell the beans and put them in a wide saucepan. Stir in the onion and olive oil. Season with salt and pepper.

Pour the water to cover beans, and simmer for 10 minutes. Add the coriander, smoked paprika, cayenne pepper, vinegar and orange zest, and cook for 5 minutes, or until the beans are soft.

Spread the beans mixture over mini-toast, transfer to a serving platter and sprinkle with parsley.

Caramelized Fruit with Nuts

(Ready in about 15 minutes | Servings 16)

Ingredients

1 cup fresh figs

1 cup apricots

3 tablespoons brown sugar

1/2 cup toasted almonds

1/2 cup toasted hazelnuts

1/2 teaspoon cinnamon

Directions

Adjust broiler rack to be about 3 inches from the flame. Set the oven to broil.

Slice the figs and apricots in halves lengthwise and press them. Sprinkle with brown sugar. Place figs and apricots in a single layer on a baking sheet.

Broil until the fruits are caramelized, or about 5 minutes. Transfer to a serving bowl and mix with almonds and hazelnuts.

Sprinkle with cinnamon and serve with your favorite waffles.

Faux Butter Crackers

(Ready in about 30 minutes | Servings 6)

Ingredients

1 cup all-purpose flour

1/3 cup nutritional yeast

1 teaspoon fine sea salt

1/2 teaspoon black pepper

4 tablespoons non-dairy butter

1/4 cup almond milk

dried herbs of choice

Directions

Combine the flour, yeast, salt, pepper and your favorite herbs. Place the faux non-diary butter on top and combine by using a mixer, till the mixture has the appearance of a coarse meal. Add the almond milk, 1 tablespoon at a time, and mix to make a dough for crackers.

Preheat the oven to 350 degrees F. Line baking sheets with parchment paper

Cut out shapes by using small cookie cutters. Repeat this process until you run out of dough.

Place the crackers on the prepared baking sheets. There are about 30 crackers. Bake for 17 minutes, or until the crackers are golden brown.

Savory Mediterranean Muffins

(Ready in about 40 minutes | Servings 12)

Ingredients

2 teaspoons lemon juice

1½ cups) unsweetened soymilk

3 tablespoons ground flaxseed

¼ cup water

2 cups pastry flour

1 cup cornmeal

1 teaspoon salt

1 teaspoon baking soda

1/4 cup olive oil

1 tablespoon dried basil

1 teaspoon dried dill

1/2 teaspoon ground black pepper

8 sun-dried tomatoes in oil, finely chopped

16 olives, chopped

Non-stick cooking spray if required

Directions

Preheat the oven to 350 degrees F. Coat a muffin pan with non-stick spray.

Combine the lemon juice and soymilk in a mixing bowl. Add the flaxseed and water. Set aside.

Mix together the flour, cornmeal, salt, and baking soda in another mixing bowl.

Add the oil, basil, dill and pepper, and whisk until all ingredients are well combined.

Add the wet mixture into the dry mixture. Then add chopped tomatoes and chopped olives. The dough is ready now.

Divide the dough among the muffin cups and bake for 18 minutes. You can check with toothpick if this is done.

Remove the muffins from the oven and let cool on a wire rack.

Chick-Wheat Muffins

(Ready in about 40 minutes | Servings 24)

Ingredients

1 cup chickpea flour

3 cups whole wheat pastry flour

4 teaspoons garam masala,

2 teaspoons dried chili peppers, crushed

1 teaspoon baking powder

1 teaspoon baking soda

2 teaspoons salt

1/2 cup (128 g) tahini

1/4 cup sesame oil

1 tablespoon juice from fresh lemon

2 ½ cups almond non-dairy milk

Directions

Preheat the oven to 350 degrees F. Line muffin pans with paper liners.

Combine together the flours, garam masala, chili peppers, baking powder, baking soda, and salt. Reserve.

In another bowl, whisk the tahini, oil, lemon juice and almond milk.

Combine the wet ingredients with the dry ingredients, do not overmix.

Divide the batter among the muffin pans and bake for 18 minutes.

You can cover them with a foil to prevent burning.

Remove from the pan and cool completely before storing. Serve with your favorite vegan sauce.

Walnut and Cranberry Veganzola Balls

(Ready in about 40 minutes | Servings 16)

Ingredients

1 ½ cup tofu ricotta

2 tablespoons canola olive oil

2 tablespoons flax meal

2 tablespoons (30 ml) warm water

1 tablespoon miso

2 teaspoons garlic powder

1 jalapeño, minced

1 teaspoon liquid smoke

1 cup (120 g) walnuts, broken into small pieces

1/2 cup cranberries

Salt to taste

Black pepper to taste

Directions

Drain and press the tofu. Combine tofu with canola oil, flax meal, water, miso, garlic powder, jalapeño and liquid smoke. Mix till all ingredients are combined well.

Stir in the walnut pieces and cranberries, and season with salt and pepper. Taste and adjust the seasonings.

Shape your mixture into equal balls and serve.

Coconut Banana Muffins

(Ready in about 40 minutes | Servings 16)

Ingredients

1 cup shredded coconut

3/4 cup instant oats

1 cup whole wheat pastry flour

1/2 teaspoon salt

1 teaspoon baking powder

1/2 teaspoon baking soda

1/4 cup margarine, melted

1/3 cup brown sugar

2 tablespoons molasses

1 banana

3 tablespoons non-dairy milk

1/2 teaspoon cinnamon

1/3 cup non-dairy chocolate, grated or chocolate curls

Nonstick cooking spray

Directions

Preheat the oven to 350 degrees F. Lightly coat a muffin pan with non-stick spray.

Combine the coconut, oats, flour, salt, baking powder and baking soda in a large mixing bowl.

Blend the melted margarine, sugar, molasses, banana, milk and cinnamon until the mixture is smooth.

To make a dough for muffins, merge wet and dry mixture. Stir in the chocolate curls.

Divide the dough among the muffin cups and bake for 20 minutes, or until a toothpick that is inserted into the center of a muffin comes out clean.

Arrange on a large serving platter and decorate with coconut flakes.

Coffee Jumbo Muffins

(Ready in about 40 minutes | Servings 12)

Ingredients

4 ½ cup whole wheat flour

1 teaspoon baking powder

1 teaspoon baking soda

1/2 teaspoon kosher salt

4 teaspoons instant espresso powder

1/4 cup unsweetened cocoa powder

1/4 cup blended silken tofu

3/4 cup sugar

1/4 cup margarine

1 cup plus unsweetened non-dairy milk

1 teaspoon Allspice

1/2 teaspoon Cardamom, ground

2 tablespoons Sucanat

2 tablespoons margarine

Directions

Preheat the oven to 350 degrees F. Prepare jumbo muffin pan.

Mix together the flour, baking powder, and salt to combine well.

Blend the espresso powder, cocoa powder, tofu, sugar, margarine, milk, allspice and cardamom.

To make a dough: place wet ingredients into the dry ingredients, and do not overmix.

Place the dough equally among the muffin cups.

To make the topping decoration: Sprinkle 1/2 teaspoon Sucanat and then place 1/2 teaspoon of margarine on top of each muffin. Bake for 18 minutes, or until the muffins are golden browned.

Banana Cookies with Jam

(Ready in about 40 minutes | Servings 16)

Ingredients

2 cups rolled oats

2 large mashed banana

3 tablespoons ground flax seed

1 tablespoon sesame seeds

1 teaspoon cinnamon

1/2 teaspoon grated nutmeg

1 tablespoon juice from fresh lemon

1/4 teaspoon fine grain sea salt

8 teaspoons jam

Favorite Nuts for garnish

Directions

Preheat oven to 350 degrees F. Prepare a baking sheet with parchment paper.

Blend the oats in a food processor till a coarse meal forms.

Mash the peeled banana. Stir in the seeds, cinnamon, nutmeg, lemon juice and salt to make very dense mixture.

Use favorite cake molds to form your cookies. Fill each cookie with 1 teaspoon of jam and place a nut on the top.

Bake cookies 12 minutes and chill before storing.

Quick Berry Bruschetta

(Ready in about 20 minutes | Servings 6)

Ingredients

1 baguette of Italian-style bread

1 cup berries mix of choice

1 tablespoon lemon juice

2 tablespoons olive oil

1 tablespoon fresh basil

1/2 teaspoon salt

1/4 teaspoon freshly ground black pepper

basil leaves, chopped for garnish

icing sugar, (optional)

Directions

Mix berries of choice (strawberries, raspberries, blackberries etc.) with lemon juice, oil, fresh chopped basil, salt and black pepper. Reserve.

Cut your favorite bread into 1/2-inch slices. Toast bread slices on both sides.

Transfer toasted bread slices on a platter. Spread prepared berry mixture on top of each slice of bread.

Sprinkle basil leaves and top with icing sugar if desired.

Garnish bruschetta with basil leaves if desired.

Tofu Skewers with Peanut Dipping Sauce

(Ready in about 50 minutes | Servings 4)

Ingredients

1/2 cup soy sauce

1/3 cup rice vinegar

1/3 cup) water

1 teaspoon fresh ginger, ground

2 cups firm tofu, drained and pressed

12 skewers

1/2 cup peanut butter

1/2 cup vegetable oil

2 scallions, chopped

1/4 teaspoon freshly ground black pepper

1 teaspoon paprika

Directions

Whisk together 1/3 cup soy sauce, vinegar, water and ginger in a medium mixing bowl to prepare a marinade. Reserve.

Slice prepared tofu into bite-sized pieces. Soak the tofu pieces in the prepared marinade. The tofu should marinate for about 30 minutes. Soak skewers in water for 30 minutes.

Carefully slide pieces of tofu onto the skewers.

Grill the tofu on a grill pan, for about 1 to 2 minutes each side. Transfer on a serving platter.

To make the peanut dipping sauce: Place the peanut butter, oil, scallions, remaining soy sauce, pepper and paprika in a blender and process until smooth. Pour peanut sauce over tofu skewers and serve immediately.

Galette with Vegetables and Mushrooms

(Ready in about 45 minutes | Servings 8)

Ingredients

1 ¾ cups sheet puff pastry

2 tablespoons olive oil

1 onion, sliced

1 zucchini, sliced

1 medium red pepper, seeded and sliced

1 medium yellow pepper, seeded and sliced

2 large mushrooms of choice, sliced

1/2 teaspoon kosher salt

1/4 teaspoon freshly ground black pepper

2 tablespoons tapenade

Directions

Preheat the oven to 400 degrees F.

Cut circle of pastry, then prick the whole surface of the pastry with a fork.

Place pastry on a baking sheet, and bake for 15 to 20 minutes, until the pastry is puffy.

To make a tapenade: Heat the oil in a saucepan over medium flame. Sauté the onion, zucchini and peppers, and cook for 10 minutes, until the vegetables are tender.

Add the mushrooms to the saucepan, season with salt and pepper, and cook 5 minutes.

Spread the tapenade over baked galette, layer the vegetables over it, and bake for 5 minutes more.

Sweet and Spicy Popcorn

(Ready in about 20 minutes | Servings 4)

Ingredients

1 cup popcorn kernels

3 tablespoons vegetable oil

1/4 cup vegan powdered sugar

1 tablespoon cayenne pepper

1 teaspoon paprika

1 teaspoon cinnamon

3 teaspoons fine sea salt

Directions

Heat vegetable oil in a large saucepan over high flame. Add the corn kernels and sugar, and stir well.

Cover with a lid and shake constantly once the corn kernels begin popping.

Transfer the popcorn in a large serving bowl and add cayenne, paprika, cinnamon and salt. Shake, taste and adjust the seasonings.

Download a FREE PDF file with photos of all the recipes by following the link:

21455269R00101

Printed in Great Britain
by Amazon